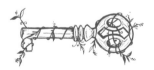

THE NEW SECRET LANGUAGE OF
DREAMS

THE NEW
SECRET LANGUAGE OF
DREAMS

THE ILLUSTRATED KEY TO UNDERSTANDING
THE MYSTERIES OF THE UNCONSCIOUS

DAVID FONTANA

WATKINS
Sharing Wisdom Since 1893

The New Secret Language of Dreams
David Fontana

This paperback edition first published in the United Kingdom
and Ireland in 2018 by Watkins, an imprint of
Watkins Media Limited
Unit 11, Shepperton House
89-93 Shepperton Road
London N1 3DF

enquiries@watkinspublishing.com

Conceived, created and designed by Watkins Media Limited

Managing Editor: Kelly Thompson
Editors: Kirsten Chapman, Ingrid Court-Jones, Jo Micklem
Managing Designer: Suzanne Tuhrim
Commissioned artwork: Karine Daisay, Penelope Dullaghan, Elliot Golden, Cecilia Carey (key motif)

British Library Cataloguing-in-Publication Data:
A CIP record for this book is available from the British Library

ISBN: 978-1-78678-232-8

10 9 8 7 6 5 4 3 2 1

Typeset in Bickham Script and MrsEaves
Color reproduction by Colourscan, Singapore
Printed in Malaysia

*"In dreaming we draw closer
to our essential nature."*

DAVID FONTANA

Contents

A Note on Dream Cues, Mood Cues and Dream Workshops:

Dream cues and **mood cues** are included alongside many of the illustrations in this book, as an aid to interpretation. They are intended to set up chains of associations and give the reader an idea of the many possible meanings that can cluster around a single dream symbol, depending on the dreamer's particular circumstances and the feelings he or she experiences in the dream.

Dream workshops are a feature of this book – there are 25 in all. Their purpose is to give practical guidance by showing dream interpretation in action on a range of real-life dreams. The names of the dreamers have been changed to preserve privacy.

1

Introducing the Dream World

Every night when we sleep, we visit an extraordinary realm where the constraints of waking logic, fact and convention cease to apply — the magical, mysterious dream world. Here, fantastic events, creatures and transformations are common. But what is their significance? And why do we dream at all? In this chapter, we begin our quest to answer these fascinating questions, as we embark on a voyage of dream discovery.

Dreams in History

Men and women almost certainly had dreams before the development of language. Early cave paintings have a dream-like quality: the animals and events they depict are often more impressionistic than naturalistic. For early humankind, in the age of pre-scientific thought, dreams and waking life probably flowed naturally into and through each other. In this early period of our existence, the boundaries between the external and internal worlds — between objective reality on the one hand, and individual experience and imagination on the other — would have been more transparent.

As the centuries progressed, people formed collective ideas about gods and spiritual beings. These beings were invisible to most people in their daily lives: they were believed to dwell in other dimensions. In dreams, of course, the normal rules of time and space do not apply — strange characters appear, bizarre things happen. So it would have been natural for our early ancestors to suppose that dreams come from beyond the self, and perhaps from the supernatural.

This should not be dismissed as mere superstition. Dreams probably played a necessary part in the inner and outer lives of early peoples. They reassured men and women that they were receiving some form of spiritual guidance — including, perhaps, warnings of impending dangers. It is even possible that some of the insights necessary to build sophisticated civilizations and to work stone and precious metals came via the same route — the dream world.

THE ANCIENT EGYPTIANS

As early as 2000 BC, the ancient Egyptians left records showing not only that information was thought to be conveyed in dreams, but also that it took cryptic form. The priesthood gained their authority partly from their skill at interpretation, and papyri from the so-called Chester Beatty Collection reveal some of the guidelines that priests used.

In a foretaste of Sigmund Freud and later psychoanalysts, one of these guidelines suggests that the images in dreams could be interpreted by association. Thus if you had dreamed of a shoe and a boat, for example, these link to ideas of travel and water, and would tell you that a journey by water was either advisable or actually lay ahead.

The Egyptian dream guidelines also referred to word similarities. If the name of a dream object resembled the term given to a completely different object, then one might stand for the other. For example, in English *rain* might suggest a *train*, or a *fan* might suggest a *man*. A further idea was that dreams might suggest their opposites — so an unhappy dream might actually indicate good fortune.

It was up to the priest to decide which of these guidelines applied in individual cases. Clearly there was nothing hard and fast about dream interpretation. The priest probably took into account personal circumstances and even the emotions aroused by the dream. Perhaps he also asked the gods for help, given that dreams were believed to arise from the spirit world, which had quite different laws from our own. Essentially, dreams were enigmatic — products of the moon and the night, themselves things of mystery.

Not only did the ancient Egyptians seek to understand dreams, they also tried to induce them. In the best-known method, the dreamer was given a potion of narcotic herbs and allowed to sleep in the temple, where the priest was on hand to offer interpretations in the morning.

Influenced by the Egyptians, the equally advanced Babylonians (from the area of modern Iraq) developed similar systems of dream analysis and inducement, as did the early Jews.

ANCIENT GREECE AND ROME

In many areas — such as the arts, philosophy and engineering — the ancient Greeks were sometimes far more advanced than we are, and none of their ideas on the nature of reality and the human mind should be dismissed too readily. The many shrines they built specifically for reading and inciting dreams are evidence of a profound knowledge of our inner life. Dreams, especially those experienced at the healing shrine at Epidaurus by Asclepius (whose snake symbol is still used today to signify the art of medicine), were also seen as a way of diagnosing and treating illness. Sometimes the god Asclepius was actually said to appear in dreams and to bestow the gift of healing on the dreamer.

In the 5th century BC, Hippocrates, one of the gifted forerunners of modern medicine, taught that healing dreams come not only from the gods but from the body itself. Deep down, our body knows what is amiss, and might even know the cure. The philosopher

Aristotle took this idea further, proposing that other bodily states might influence the content of dreams. If you have been too hot during the night, dreams of fire might result. This underlined the importance of considering all the senses when interpreting a dream: how things felt could be as important as how things looked.

The ancient Greeks and Romans also believed that dreams could mislead as well as instruct. The poets Homer, in his *Odyssey*, and later Virgil, in his *Aeneid*, give us the same vivid image. True dreams come to us through the gates of horn, while false dreams come through the gates of ivory, which are deceptive as well as beautiful — a reminder for modern dream interpreters that the most appealing analysis may not be the truest.

The dreams of the wise were believed to be sent from the gods — or God. Recurring dreams were understood to be particularly significant. Aristotle's predecessor Socrates had a dream that appeared to him at different times and in different forms throughout his life, but always with the same message: "Socrates, practise and cultivate the arts."

Opening one's mind to the Muses brought the rewards of wisdom and beauty. Socrates knew that creativity was closely linked with dreaming.

THE SACRED TRADITIONS

Dreams figure in all the major spiritual traditions. In the Hebrew Bible, God told Aaron and Miriam that if there was a true prophet among the Israelites, "I ... will speak unto him in a dream." Job also spoke of the relationship between dreams and the Divine: "when deep sleep falleth upon men ... then He openeth the ears of men and sealeth their instruction." Dreams are equally important in the New Testament. For example, Joseph is "warned of God in a dream" about the dangers that would face his infant son, Jesus.

In Islam it is made clear that God speaks to men and women "in the form of sights or visions when the qualified recipient is asleep or in a state of trance". The Prophet himself received much of the Koran in dreams.

Tibetan Buddhism has always underlined the importance of dreaming. The Nyingma sect teaches that dreams are a dress rehearsal for death, giving us each night a foretaste of the successive stages we encounter as we die and make our transition to the afterlife. We should work to gain conscious control over the dreaming process, as this skill will enable us to have some influence over what happens when we die. If we fail in this, after death we will be carried along by the force of our karma (the impact of our past actions on future lives), and we will miss the opportunities for spiritual development that come with dying and the immediate afterlife.

Hindu teachers have taught that the consciousness of the advanced sage runs continuously through both dreaming and dreamless sleep — the deep sleep state in which no thoughts arise but the mind remains clear and fully aware.

We find similar ideas in the Western occult traditions — the range of "hidden" beliefs and practices that includes alchemy, divination and witchcraft. Sleep, we are told, should not be wasted in a state of unconsciousness, but used as part of our spiritual journey.

SHAMANIC CULTURES

Various esoteric traditions across the world are grounded in a special sensitivity to nature and its hidden powers. Common to all is the figure of the shaman, who serves as a channel between the material and the spiritual worlds, often while in an altered state of consciousness induced by trance, drugs, rhythmic drumming and chanting — and by dreams. The latter in particular are thought to give ready access both to the elemental forces of nature (often experienced in the form of so-called power animals) and to the spirit world, where the shaman can contact the souls of the departed and learn the causes and cures of sickness within the community.

For the shaman, the spiritual world is as real as, if not more so than, the physical world — a vast dimension of infinite possibilities. The spirits are all around the living and are capable of influencing them, for good or ill. For native Australians, our physical world is even said to have been made in the Dreamtime, when the ancestral beings moved across the land, defining its physical features, populating the world, and teaching language, ceremonies and laws. However, Aboriginal people stress that the Dreamtime also continues in the present and has no foreseeable end. It is the creative force that underlies the whole of our universe.

The Science of Dreaming

Science knows *that* we dream — we have objective evidence from the changes in brain rhythm it causes — but it is not certain *why* we dream. It is accepted that dreaming appears to have a psychological and probably a physical purpose, but precisely what that purpose is remains a matter of debate. As in so many areas of the mind and its secrets, science still has much to learn.

THE LEVELS OF SLEEP

There is agreement, however, on the mechanics of sleeping and dreaming. Much of what we have learnt has come from work in sleep laboratories, where volunteers are wired up to equipment that monitors their brain activity, heartbeat, muscular activity and eye movements while they sleep. Results show that we experience different stages or levels of sleep during the course of the night. Within the first hour of sleep, we disengage increasingly from the outside world, descending through three successively deepening levels of sleep, until we reach the fourth and deepest level. At this stage our breathing is slow and rhythmic; our blood pressure, heart rate and body temperature are lowered; physical movement virtually stops; and our brainwaves decrease from between four and eight cycles per minute to between a half and two cycles per minute.

Around 30 minutes later, things alter again, and we move upwards through the levels until we return to Level One. Many of the physiological changes associated with Level Four are reversed; the functions of the brain and heart appear much nearer to the waking state, while the body becomes more active and the eyes are seen to move around behind the closed eyelids. These rapid eye movements give us the term *REM sleep*.

At this stage we seem on the verge of waking, though, strangely, it is actually often harder to wake people up at this point — hence this level is sometimes also called "paradoxical sleep". So different is this state, both from waking and deep sleep, that some authorities regard it as a distinct state of being, a suggestion reinforced by the fact that this is the point at which we usually experience our first episode of vivid dreaming.

Normally, this first stage of REM sleep lasts no longer than five to 10 minutes, after which we return to deeper levels of sleep, though rarely to Level Four again. Subsequently,

REM and so-called NREM (non-rapid eye movement) sleep alternate throughout the night, with usually four to seven repetitions of the cycle. The REM episodes tend to be longer each time, culminating in a period of 20 to 40 minutes just before waking.

The average adult spends a total of around one and a half hours in REM sleep each night. This tends to diminish as we grow older, while newborn babies pass some 60 percent of their sleep in this state. (Are they dreaming, and, if so, of what? Unfortunately, they can't tell us.) There is even evidence that we may dream during parts of NREM sleep, though the dreams are of a different kind. In REM sleep they tend to be vivid and active, while in NREM sleep they are more shadowy and indistinct. Some dreamers describe NREM dreams as taking place in a muffled, fog-bound world, characterized by dim shapes and low levels of energy.

THE FUNCTION OF DREAMS

Even people who claim never to experience dreams are usually able to describe them if they are woken during REM sleep. This suggests two things: firstly that these people simply fail to remember their other dreams; and secondly that dreams are in themselves universal and therefore no doubt perform

REM SLEEP

If you watch someone who is in REM sleep, you can see their eyes moving behind their eyelids. They may in fact be watching the events in their dreams — subjects who have been woken during REM sleep have reported dream activity consistent with their eye movements. Also, we know that some of the brain activity during REM dreams is similar to the kind that would occur if the dream events were actually happening.

If you have difficulty remembering your dreams, ask someone to wake you during REM sleep, or set an alarm to go off about an hour and a half after you fall asleep. You can even buy a special eye mask that senses the onset of REM sleep. A light flashes within the mask, bright enough to alert you that you are dreaming, but not bright enough to waken you. There is a good chance you will then remember the dream.

an essential function, even if we do not remember them.

What might this function be? Broadly speaking, there are two categories of explanations: physiological and analytical. Physiological theories propose that physical processes within the brain are responsible for instigating dreams. For example, one view is that the brain-stem randomly fires signals into higher areas of the brain, which then use stored memories to make sense of these incoming signals – a process that helps to maintain and reinforce these memories. Another idea belonging to this group is that dreams are the brain's way of processing and consolidating the events of waking life and discarding unwanted material.

Physiological theories maintain that dream content is illogical simply because during sleep we are unable to relate what is happening inside our heads to real events in the outside world. According to this view, although dreaming is associated with useful brain activity, dream content is essentially unimportant.

The various physiological theories fail to explain why dreams often contain a strong narrative content. Rather than being a disconnected and confused review of waking events, dreams often tell a clear and consistent story, and are able to open up new lines of thinking and reasoning. And when dreams do relate to waking events, they often transform or elaborate them, showing a strong creative element. Dreams seem to carry meaning: they excite, inspire and sometimes frighten us. Like a magic picture book, they offer us previously unimagined possibilities.

Theories in the analytical category take these facts into account and argue that, far from representing random or unwanted material, dreams provide deep insights into the workings of our mind. Thus we should learn to remember and interpret our dreams. They can help us not only to understand the sources of our instincts, impulses and ideas, but also to make better use of our potential. This reminds us of the theories of the ancient Greeks: dreams may not be sent by the gods, but they still have the power to instruct and to feed our creative imagination.

THE IMPORTANCE OF DREAMS

Scientific evidence points to the fact that dreams are essential to our well-being. So vital are they, in fact, that it has been suggested that one of the reasons we sleep is in order to dream. In sleep-deprivation experiments, volunteers who have been kept awake for long periods of time begin to experience many of the phenomena of the dream state even when the brain is technically awake.

Carl Jung, one of the most important early psychologists, maintained that we actually dream 24 hours of the day, but only in sleep is our brain calm enough to be conscious of it. If true, this supports the idea that one of the functions of sleep is to allow us to become aware of our dreams, and thus to integrate dream insights into our waking life.

In other experiments volunteers have been deprived specifically of REM sleep by being aroused each time they entered the REM state. After several nights of this, their brains made more frequent attempts to experience REM sleep, and once the volunteers were allowed to sleep normally again, much of the night was devoted to REM sleep, even at the expense of deeper levels. The mind needs its quota of vivid dreaming, and, if necessary, it will seek to make up for what it has missed.

Dreaming is fundamental to our lives, in ways we still do not fully understand. Future research will no doubt help to enlighten us.

BETWEEN WAKING AND SLEEPING

If you observe yourself in the process of falling asleep, you may be aware of a strange half-world between waking and sleeping, in which you may catch glimpses of strange images or experience a wide range of ideas. Yet coming back to full wakefulness, you remember little or nothing of these thoughts. This is known as the *hypnagogic* state. Many renowned artists have reported receiving fantastic visions during these states. Salvador Dalí, the surrealist painter who married images of dreams with images of reality, trained himself to enter and extend his hypnagogic awareness to gain material for his work.

Mysteries of the Mind

The mind and the universe itself are full of mysteries, and it may be that we can never fathom these so long as we remain trapped within our earthly perspective. That we should exist at all, as individuals and as a species, is one of the deepest mysteries of all. And within that, the nature of the mind poses some of the most intriguing questions. We live in physical bodies and the brain is a physical organ, yet the mind consists of thoughts, memories, emotions, motives, hopes, fears, anxieties, happiness and dreams, all of which are non-physical. Even those who claim that the mind is no more than the sum of the brain's functions cannot explain how the electrochemical activity of the brain can produce the non-physical theatre of the mind. The psychospiritual traditions (the world's great religions), and even certain leading neurologists and brain scientists, argue that the mind cannot be found within the brain, and that the mind may even be some sort of non-physical aspect of our being that works *through* the brain, using it as the connection between the non-physical and the physical self. This notion obviously links to the idea of a soul and to life beyond physical death.

THE CONSCIOUS AND THE UNCONSCIOUS MIND

One of the greatest secrets of the mind is, as Carl Jung tells us, that we do not know where it ends. We "live" in only a small part of the mind, the conscious mind, which is essentially the part that governs the normal actions of everyday life. We are "conscious" of the world around us, of our thoughts, of making choices, of liking or disliking things, of trying to make sense of life, and of experiencing emotions such as love, compassion and empathy. But there is much more to the mind than this.

Where do thoughts come from? One moment the mind is blank, the next moment a thought arrives. Where was it before it arrived? If it did not exist, how was it formed? At some hidden level the thought was created and brought to our attention. So what is this level? We don't know. We invent a term for it, the *unconscious*, but a term is not an explanation. The arrival of thoughts demonstrates to us that the unconscious exists, yet we know very little about it. However, during sleep our conscious mind closes down, and we move into the unconscious, where we experience the strange dreams it creates for us.

Two of the most brilliant explorers of the unconscious, Freud and Jung, recognized that the unconscious contains three distinct levels, all of which are essential to our understanding of dreams. These are:

The preconscious
This consists of the vast store of facts and memories that are not in the conscious mind at any one moment but can readily be called up whenever we want them.

The personal unconscious
This also contains thousands of facts and memories, but ones that we appear to have forgotten — they can be recalled only in special circumstances.

The collective unconscious
This is a hidden reservoir of thought common to and potentially accessible by everyone, regardless of culture. It was recognized by Jung as lying below the personal unconscious (see p. 21).

THE PRECONSCIOUS AND THE PERSONAL UNCONSCIOUS

The *preconscious*, which we are accessing all the time in order to live our daily lives, is easy enough to understand, but the *personal unconscious* is more complex. We can illustrate its workings by thinking about what happens when we visit a place we knew well as a child,

SIGMUND FREUD (1856–1939)

As the inventor of psychoanalysis, Freud is also credited with introducing Western science to the psychological importance of dreams. After qualifying as a medical doctor, Freud turned his attention to the study of neurosis and of the mind's mysteries. In his classic book *The Interpretation of Dreams* (1900), he suggested that dreams provide the best clues to the content of the unconscious mind, which in his view was the source of most psychological problems.

Freud argued that dreams are essentially an "acting out" of repressed emotions, and particularly those to do with sexual desires. Their content is largely symbolic because much of it would shock the conscious mind into wakefulness if it were more explicit.

Freud believed that the meanings contained in dreams are best identified through a process of *free association*, in which the client provides a chain of associations for each dream symbol.

but to which we have not returned for some years. From the moment we see those once-familiar sights, we seem to recapture the lost experiences and emotions of childhood. We notice things that have changed and remember them as they used to be. We recall long-forgotten faces, long-forgotten scenes (on walks perhaps), and the voices of long-forgotten companions. All these memories have been stored away in the personal unconscious, where they have lain untouched for years. Similar things happen when we come upon faded photographs of family holidays from years ago.

For both Freud and Jung, as well as the psychologists and psychiatrists who continue today to carry out their methods of psychotherapy, many (perhaps most) of our psychological problems have their origin in the early years of our lives. Experiences with parents, with teachers, with other children, in fact with all the people and events in our childhood, leave their mark upon us – for both good and bad. Many of our attitudes, interests and inclinations have their origin in these experiences. So do many of our dislikes and, more importantly, our anxieties and complexes. Stored deep within the personal

CARL JUNG (1875–1961)

A medical doctor and early collaborator with Freud, Jung was one of the finest minds to study psychology. He disagreed with the importance Freud attached to sexual repression, believing that much of our motivation comes from a deeper, more spiritual source. Like Freud, Jung considered dreams to provide the best insights into the unconscious, but unlike Freud, he saw dreams as creative and visionary, not simply as wish-fulfilments.

The method Jung developed for working with clients suffering from psychological problems is commonly known as analytical psychotherapy. In this still widely used practice, a therapist encourages a client, among other things, to talk through the archetypal material of their dreams to gain increased self-awareness. Jung's work is also important for transpersonal psychology, which studies spiritual and mystical states and their significance for our lives.

unconscious is the source of much of who we are. By accessing the content of the personal unconscious — spontaneously in dreams or through techniques such as psychotherapy and hypnosis — we can help ourselves to understand the mysteries of our own being.

THE COLLECTIVE UNCONSCIOUS

Going deeper into the unconscious, Jung recognized a third level below the personal unconscious, which he called the *collective unconscious*. Evidence from history, from across cultures and from the unconscious material brought to the surface during psychotherapy suggests strongly that far from being individual and personal like the two higher levels, the collective unconscious is shared by us all. It is, in fact, the common inherited basis of our psychological life, just as our biology is the common inherited basis of our physical life. And it is to the collective unconscious that the statement "We do not know where the mind ends" refers.

The collective unconscious extends not only across the human race and across history, it appears also to extend into dimensions that are best described as spiritual and mystical. Through it we have access to infinite possibilities. It is from the collective unconscious that many of our more profound creative insights and imaginative works emerge — art, architecture, music, poetry, and much else besides. It may be through the collective unconscious that we find our pathway to the divine.

ARCHETYPES AND THE COLLECTIVE UNCONSCIOUS

The collective unconscious teems with formless psychological energies. This means that they can be drawn to our attention only if they emerge into the mind as symbols — that is, images that represent some deep-rooted quality or motivation. Recognizing such a symbol when we come across it enables us to identify the energies it embodies. Many of these symbols, which Jung referred to as *archetypes* (a term first used by the 1st-century philosopher Philo Judaeus of Alexandria), take the form, for example, of wise or heroic men and women, fabulous beasts, or gods and goddesses. The most significant manifestations of such figures or creatures appear in the myths and legends of the world, as well as in fairy stories. Although largely fictional, these stories convey enduring truths about human nature and the human condition, and teach us profound lessons about ourselves. Jung saw that many of these tales recur in similar manifestations right across cultures, giving form to the collective unconscious through the storytelling ability of inspired men and women.

Archetypal images most frequently feature in Level Three dreams (see p.31) that occur at important transitional periods in life, such as adolescence, early parenthood and middle and old age, as well as at times of psychological and spiritual crisis. Dream archetypes can provide us with guidance and direction, sometimes warning us of possible errors of judgment, or helping us to access our deeper spiritual nature. They can open doors into the collective unconscious, allowing us to sense our intimate interconnection with our fellow humans and with the natural world, thus helping to free us from the isolation we can feel when life is not going well for us.

Archetypal dream symbols can typically be recognized by the sense of numinosity that surrounds them — that is, an ambience of awe and revelation, as if we are on the threshold of deep mysteries. They appear to take us beyond the confines of our customary psychological reality. These images are profoundly memorable, so that they stay in the mind for years.

Dreams may owe their archetypal character either to archetypal figures, such as those described below, or to archetypal events, such as shape-shifting, animals capable of speech, the sensation of flying, and supernatural experiences (for example, passing through walls and doors). Some dreamers even report mystical experiences, such as an expansion of the self that seems to embrace all reality.

Archetypes that appear specifically as male or female, as some do, in fact represent qualities we all possess and thus are equally relevant to men and women alike.

One way of opening the mind to archetypal dreams is to study and meditate on pictures of archetypes, such as those of the Tarot cards. Allow them to "communicate" with you — that is, to stimulate your own creative thoughts and ideas in relation to them. Hold dialogues with them if you can, and try to keep them in your mind as you fall asleep.

The *Wise Old Man* archetype appears in dreams typically as a magician, a teacher or any other figure of authority, including a

guide or a celestial being. He symbolizes a primal source of wisdom and creative vitality, which can heal or destroy in order to make way for change and development.

The *Hero* plays a significant role in many of the great myths of the world. This figure represents our striving toward the good and the noble, and also the questing, searching side of us that seeks answers to life's fundamental questions. Often a dream where a psychological or physical challenge takes place will involve the Hero archetype.

The *Earth (or Great) Mother* represents nurture, fertility and Earth's deep mysteries. But, like many archetypes, she can also have a negative side — that of the dominating, possessive mother or the weaver of spells, who rob others of the power of independent action. Hugely significant in our psychological and spiritual development, she embodies much of the essence of feminine mystery and power.

The *Divine Child* symbolizes rebirth, innocence, the uncorrupted wisdom that represents the dawn of new opportunities; also, our striving for individuality, wholeness and freedom from greed and the selfish ego.

The *Beautiful Young Girl* symbolizes intuitive wisdom and access to many of life's mysteries. She complements the Hero by showing him the path to follow and by providing some of the symbolic objects (such as a key or talisman) that he needs to complete his quest.

The *Trickster* is the archetype of everything that upsets humanity's best-laid plans, but he will exhibit both a dark and a light side. The joker and shape-shifter, he can be malicious but often forces us to reappraise our established ways of thinking.

The *Shadow* represents our dark side, the things that we do not want to be or cannot face in ourselves. It takes the form of a silent, unsettling presence or hostile companion, and often elicits strong feelings of fear or anger from the dreamer. By acknowledging the Shadow we can potentially deal with it, and transform some of its negative energies into something positive.

The *Persona* may take the form of a vaguely familiar stranger or perhaps a scarecrow or tramp. It is the mask we adopt to face the world — a compromise between who we are and what others expect of us. The Persona becomes harmful if we mistake it for our real self.

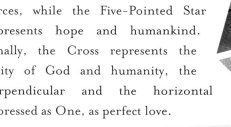

The *Anima,* which is sometimes synonymous with the Beautiful Young Girl, represents the feminine intuition inherent in both men and women, but often neglected by the former. She acts as a guide for the dreamer, revealing how to explore the inner self in new ways, encouraging wisdom and self-knowledge.

The *Animus* represents the masculine energies that exist within the female, sometimes appearing in dreams as the Hero. He symbolizes the assertive, courageous qualities that women do not always realize they possess. Through self-exploration these values can be accessed and absorbed into the waking self.

Geometrical Shapes can also be archetypes, of a kind that is easy to recognize. The Circle symbolizes wholeness and completion, an integration of the beginning and the end, and ultimately the first cause, the Divine. The Square denotes solidity, the four directions, the four elements, and Earth itself. The Upward-Pointing Triangle represents our spiritual aspirations, and the Downward-Pointing Triangle the outpouring of spiritual sustenance for the world. The Six-Pointed Star symbolizes the blending of these two forces, while the Five-Pointed Star represents hope and humankind. Finally, the Cross represents the unity of God and humanity, the perpendicular and the horizontal expressed as One, as perfect love.

OTHER DREAM PIONEERS

Many other psychologists have contributed methods of dream interpretation. One of the most notable, Fritz Perls, the founder of Gestalt Therapy, believed that dreams symbolize unfinished emotional business, and that dream characters and objects can be projections of the dreamer's self. Perls developed role-play techniques in which he suggested that his clients "address" dream characters or objects, then change roles to provide their replies. By contrast, the Swiss psychiatrist Medard Boss downplayed symbolism and the unconscious, instead arguing that dreams are open expressions of conscious desires. As such, they should be taken more at face value, an approach that concentrates on Level One dreams rather than Levels Two and Three (see pp.28–31).

Dream Workshop No. 1

The Dreamer

Peter, 35, is a successful advertising executive, who can afford a luxurious lifestyle. After a recent family holiday in Africa, he feels that he would like to work in a job that helps those less fortunate than himself, but he is procrastinating about actually making the change, mainly because he is worried about uprooting his wife and son.

THE DREAM

Peter is setting off on a business trip and gets into a taxi to go to the train station. On arrival there he finds that it has changed into a circus. Amid all the excitement and the chaos, he can't find the ticket counter and he feels anxious about missing his train. He dodges in and out of acrobats and jugglers in his search for the ticket office. Then he sees an old man sitting on a bench, beckoning to him. He goes over to the old man, who picks up a newspaper to read. He sits down next to him. Suddenly, the station changes into a tranquil garden. Peter feels at home here, peaceful and quiet, and catching the train is no longer a priority.

INTERPRETATION

The dream appears to start with straightforward, everyday realism. Peter is setting off on a business trip and he takes a **Taxi** instead of public transport, reflecting his affluent lifestyle. He arrives at the **Train Station**, a typical symbol for travel but also for a change of direction.

Such a change does in fact occur, and the dream seems to become more symbolic when Peter finds himself in a **Circus**. The circus is often a childhood symbol for magic or transformation, but this one contains **Acrobats** and **Jugglers**, who are performing skills that are beyond Peter himself and may represent feelings of inadequacy on his part (Peter should ask himself whether he feels that his profession is of less value than an occupation in which he could help others). In spite of the fact that the station has become a circus, Peter still searches for the ticket office and worries about missing his train. Perhaps he is reluctant or unable to acknowledge the change that has taken place around him (or, in fact, within him).

The dream then undergoes another transformation, introducing a more resonant symbol: the **Old Man**. This figure may symbolize the archetypal Wise Old Man, a source of teaching and wisdom, while his **Newspaper** represents the knowledge he has to share. Peter joins the old man on the **Bench**, a location that suggests reassurance and solidity. Then suddenly the scene becomes a **Peaceful Garden**. This pleasant change might indicate that Peter is ready to open himself up to new wisdom and will find contentment in doing so. His train, vital to his working life, ceases to be a priority.

On the face of it, the dream seems to be telling Peter that he should join one of the caring professions — that this is what he wants deep down. Of course, this guidance is given at the emotional level, but real life also has to take account of economic factors, as well as the well-being of his family. This is particularly true if Peter's work ambitions lead them to move to a more impoverished country. All these factors Peter must consider: he cannot make his decision based solely on his dreams.

*A*rchetypal dreams are most likely to occur at transitional points in our lives, but they rarely tell us exactly what to do. Here the Wise Old Man may be a source of personal growth and energy — what Jung called a "mana" personality. But the impulse to personal growth, promoted by a dream, often has to give way to the demands of love and familial responsibility.

Three Levels of Dreams

If the unconscious consists of three progressively deeper levels, it follows that dreams may arise from each of these levels, and vary accordingly in their character and significance. Understanding this can help us with our effort of interpretation. In this book we refer to dreams originating from the preconscious as Level One dreams, those from the personal unconscious as Level Two, and the far less frequent dreams from the collective unconscious as Level Three. However, it is possible for one dream to contain elements from all three levels.

DREAMS FROM THE PRECONSCIOUS (LEVEL ONE)

Once you begin to study your dreams, you will probably become aware of some that draw recognizably upon events from your day or in recent memory — even though various distortions may also be introduced. Many dreams from the preconscious relate simply to interesting, amusing or perhaps upsetting things that have happened. They may touch on important issues, things that are making us happy or concerned. However, it is no contradiction to suggest that at the same time the unconscious may simply be reviewing events, following unfinished lines of thought, much as the conscious mind does during the day. The review may usefully draw attention to key details since forgotten, so even dreams that seem to skim the surface of the preconscious may be much more than transient nonsense.

We may find it puzzling that our dreams have focused on seemingly trivial events. But if we accept that dreams are likely to be in some way meaningful then the question of why we dream of a particular incident becomes highly relevant. We may find the answer if we focus upon what precisely the dream brings to mind.

Let us say that you have dreamed of a house that you walked past during the day but barely noticed. You might start dream interpretation by picturing that house in your mind's eye. It then occurs to you that there is something curiously familiar about the building. The more you think about it, the more the sense of familiarity grows, until suddenly you realize that it reminds you of a friend's house where you went to a party as a child. Suddenly, you remember who opened the front door, the welcome you received, and individual incidents at the party. Maybe you met a child of the opposite sex and felt the first strange stirrings of sexual attraction. You now recall the appearance of the other child, and whether they liked you in return.

These memories may carry with them some of the feelings you actually had at the time — a sense of emotional fragility, for example. How easily hurt many children are by any hint of rejection, how deeply touched by any act of kindness! You may also recognize that you have never quite come to terms with your vulnerability, and that this has perhaps led your adult self to distance itself from others, to protect your feelings by developing an emotional shield. It may be time to try to let go of this protection, which may have prevented you from enjoying relationships to your fullest capacity. In this way even a Level One dream can lead to Level Two and open up a portal of self-understanding.

It is always relevant to ask why, out of the many experiences of a day, our minds chose to dream about one in particular. Certainly it is worth looking for links to long-forgotten experiences that have helped to shape the people we have become. Such experiences may have been repressed by the conscious mind, pushed deep into the unconscious soon after they occurred because they were too painful or too incomprehensible to be accommodated at such a young age.

DREAMS FROM THE PERSONAL UNCONSCIOUS (LEVEL TWO)

The memories contained in the preconscious are full of gaps, but the personal unconscious knows far more about us and about our past, stretching right back into our earliest experiences. It has even been suggested that we forget nothing that happens to us in our lifetimes, and people who have been close to death sometimes say that their past lives flashed before them, condensed into seconds yet containing every detail. In tapping into such rich sources of information, dreams from the personal unconscious can give us valuable insights into who we are today, revealing aspects of our nature that are holding us back, as well as abilities and desires that can drive us in the future.

Some dreams that come from the personal unconscious may relate to unresolved experiences from our childhood. Ambivalent feelings of love and anger toward parents, the fear and confusion of certain events, or the shame produced by humiliating incidents or early sexual arousal are all difficult to deal with in childhood. The young mind may defend itself by pushing these feelings down into the unconscious. But this does not make them vanish. Repressed emotions lurk beneath the surface of our lives and can make sudden reappearances in adulthood, causing inexplicable feelings of depression, poor self-confidence, anxiety, guilt, self-blame and so on. We may even develop strange phobias.

Dreams relating to repressed emotions may be disturbing and even nightmarish. We may be menaced by unseen forces, held under water by giant hands, pursued by terrifying men; or we may witness acts of brutality. Some people's nightmares make them afraid of falling asleep. But even the worst dreams have a purpose: to bring unresolved traumas and haunting memories to our attention so that we can start dealing with them.

We are less prone to repress unwanted material in adult life, but we may engage in another form of self-protection, namely denial. We may be strongly attracted to someone else's partner, or feel hostility toward a family member. We may have doubts about our ability to do our jobs effectively, or about the true nature of our religious or political beliefs. If we attempt to deceive ourselves and others by denying that these issues exist, the unconscious may bring them back to our attention in our dreams. A requirement of psychological health is honesty to ourselves, and only by facing up to our problems do we have a good chance of resolving them or living in peace with them.

Happily, dreams from the personal unconscious can also be very pleasant. They may recall good times we have experienced or enable us to relive the high spirits of our childhood. Roving freely across time and place, they remind us that nothing of value is ever lost, including the wisdom we have acquired during our lives. Such dreams may also draw our attention to abilities we have never fully appreciated, and may help us to unlock new talents and interests.

Some people claim that their Level Two dreams are almost always unpleasant. However, volunteers who are awoken during REM sleep in laboratories actually tend to report a high incidence of pleasant or emotionally neutral dreams. Once we teach ourselves to remember dreams, we begin to take more notice of the pleasant ones. More importantly, we begin to appreciate our dreams more fully, as they become more vibrant and exciting, more intriguing and stimulating; and they literally offer a new dimension to our experience.

DREAMS FROM THE COLLECTIVE UNCONSCIOUS (LEVEL THREE)

Jung referred to dreams from the collective unconscious as "grand" or "great" dreams. Far rarer than Level One and Two dreams — some of us may have only a few in our lives — grand dreams have a profound effect on us and remain clear in the memory. They seem to originate from a source outside of us, imparting wisdom that could come only from other minds or a higher power.

This message may be conveyed through an archetypal figure (see pp.21–25). Alternatively, a grand dream might use a person known to us as its messenger, perhaps even someone who has died. For centuries, people have reported meeting in a dream a dead loved one who reassures the dreamer of their survival into the afterlife. Some have given evidence of the psychic reality of their experiences by providing facts that could not have been learned by "normal" means (see pp.160–163). Phenomena such as precognition, clairvoyance and telepathy might be explained in part by the collective unconscious — a pool of consciousness that all human beings share, which may embrace minds other than our own.

Whether they enable us to tap into an innate, personal spirituality or allow us to connect in other ways with the divine, grand dreams can be valuable vehicles for spiritual development. Their force can be disturbing if they challenge set beliefs or ways of being, and suggest a need for important change in our lives. More often such dreams elicit feelings of deep joy, assuring us that we are an essential part of a larger whole, in which we each have an important part to play.

Dream Workshop No. 2

The Dreamer

Stuart is thoroughly enjoying his twenties, socializing among many friends, with no plans to settle down and no worries about the meaning of life. He is a successful IT consultant and a high earner.

THE DREAM

A swan flies down at sunset to land on a beautiful lake, among flocks of ducks and other water birds, as well as fishermen in rowing boats. There's a loud beating of wings and a big splash, which makes all the other birds fly off and all the boats capsize, so the fishermen have to swim to the bank. The swan disappears under the water but doesn't re-surface. There is a period of worried suspense. Still the swan doesn't appear. Stuart starts thinking about what he could do if the swan's wings were so drenched with water that she – he thinks of the swan as female – couldn't fly any more. He's sitting on one of the overturned boats, with his computer in front of him. He internet-searches the term "swan song", but the entries are impossible to read in the fading light. He looks down into the water and sees that there are lots of computer mice, with long tails, swimming furiously like eels or tadpoles just below the water's surface.

THE INTERPRETATION

The initial part of this narrative suggests elements of a Level Three dream, the deepest level of dreaming: the **Swan** is a symbol of beauty, majesty and sexuality; the **Sunset** represents the descent into the underworld of the unconscious; and **Amphibious Birds** connect the elements of water and air, the respective domains of the unconscious and of the spirit. The presence of **Fishermen**, an enduring symbol of those who reach deep into the unconscious in search of wisdom, further strengthens this suggestion.

All seems well until the **Big Splash** interrupts the scene, probably representing Stuart's critical and perhaps sceptical mind. The birds take flight and the fishermen abandon their task and seek the "security" of the shore. However, Stuart remains, albeit in a precarious position on an **Upturned Rowing boat**.

Stuart is concerned for the swan. If one goes deep into the unconscious, will one return to normality? He tries to solve things through rational thinking – represented by his **Computer** – but finds that this cannot provide him with the answer. He looks into the water, but instead of seeing **Fish** (the natural inhabitants of the deep and a symbol of fertility and renewal), he sees **Computer Mice**, manmade objects that are out of their element.

The contrast between the beautiful scene at the outset and the sterility of the computer and computer mice is striking. Stuart tells others he has no "worries about the meaning of life", yet the dream seems to be telling him that there is more to life than modern technology.

*D*reams often use wordplay: they can be clever punsters. Here the word "mouse"
in a computer context has suggested the parallel meaning of a wild creature,
so the dream wittily places the computer device in a natural setting. Its function is to
suggest that this dreamer might be approaching life with too much logical analysis.

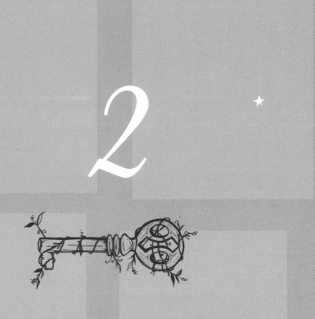

2

Basic Dream Skills

On waking we may feel confident we won't forget our dreams — yet often, just an hour or two later, they have maddeningly vanished. This chapter provides simple techniques that will help you to remember more of your dreams, describes common dream types and dream content, and outlines various methods for interpretation. The first step toward discovering the riches of our unconscious is simply to recognize that dreams are worth recalling.

The Art of Dream Retention

We may all dream for up to two hours every night, but many people say that they never remember even a single dream. Why? The mind obviously has to be able to distinguish between dreams and reality, so as we surface from sleep we appear to go through a process that ensures that we recall dreams in a different way from waking events. Add to this the fact that, from early childhood onward, we are taught not to take dreams seriously, and it's not surprising that our natural ability to remember them becomes increasingly inhibited.

Luckily, you can restore this ability with the most basic dream skills, which can be summarized as follows:

1. *Make friends with your dreams.*

2. *Take active steps to remember them.*

3. *Be mindful in waking life.*

To "make friends with your dreams" means to regard them as an essential part of your mental life. Welcome them and feel grateful for them. Recognize that they are worth recalling, and get this message through to your unconscious by repeating "I will remember my dreams" to yourself during the day, and particularly as you sink into sleep at night. Also, acknowledge that

while some dream material is rather like the inconsequential thinking in which we indulge during the day, much of it is an important link between the conscious mind and the two deeper levels of the unconscious mind — the personal and the collective unconscious.

The second essential is to train yourself to remember your dreams. Lie still upon waking, as your body is likely to be in the position it was in during the last stage of dreaming. Keep your eyes closed, and avoid thinking about the coming day or other concerns. When the adventures of the night have come back to you, note them in a dream diary (keep this within easy reach of your bed). The very act of writing dreams down helps to fix them in the memory, but if you forget them you can always return to the diary. Refrain from interpreting your dreams as you note them — this can come later. Interpretation engages your conscious mind and may inhibit further dream recall or actually distort dream memories. If associations spring immediately to mind, well and good, but don't seek them. For the same reason, don't label dreams as pleasant or unpleasant, or try to identify which level of the unconscious they come from. For now, they are simply dreams.

Also, you should try to notice any special circumstances that assist dream recall. People often report remembering dreams more readily on vacation — probably because they are more relaxed and unhurried — or when they sleep in a certain position, take a siesta or get more sleep before midnight, and so on. Make good use of whatever assists your dream recall, whenever possible.

The third skill to learn is the art of paying attention, often called mindfulness. Take more notice of what is going on around you during the day, rather than getting lost in the mental chatter that usually claims our attention. Meditation can also improve mindfulness. A simple exercise involves spending a few minutes each day, ideally at the same time, sitting quietly and focusing on your breathing. Focus either on the point where your breath enters and leaves the nose or on the rising and falling of your abdomen. If your mind wanders, bring it gently back to your breathing. As you improve your powers of concentration, this will be carried over into your dreams, making you more alert to dream events. This skill is important if you want to explore more advanced dream experiences (see Chapter 6).

Common Dream Content

The dream researcher Dr. Calvin Hall collected samples of more than 10,000 dreams from the general population in order to identify the most commonly occurring themes. His work showed that, although there are cultural variations, the dreams of people around the world are more similar in their themes than they are different. However, each of us seems to experience a particular set of themes, which recur in our dreams over time with regular frequency.

SETTINGS

Hall's samples showed that in terms of where dreams took place, houses and other buildings were at the top of the list, with living rooms the most frequent setting, followed by bedrooms, kitchens, stairs, and cellars or basements. Places of work appear less often than domestic premises. Interpretations varied from dreamer to dreamer, but it was discovered that many people associate houses with themselves, while the different rooms reveal particular aspects of their lives. The living room may represent the public, shared self, and the bedroom the deeper, more private self. The kitchen may symbolize needs and tastes, the stairs the progress made in relevant areas of life, and the cellar or basement the often concealed and perhaps even disturbing areas of the unconscious.

PEOPLE

Only around a fifth of the characters in dreams were family members, while more than a third were friends or acquaintances and almost half were strangers (only one percent were famous people). A possible explanation for this is that there is less need to dream about family, as we are generally aware of our feelings toward them, whereas we may be more intrigued by friends or strangers. Women tended to dream equally of both sexes, while men dreamed twice as often of other men as of women. This may be because men feel more competition with other men, and express these feelings in dreams. In 15 percent of dreams, the dreamer was alone.

ACTIONS

Hall's research revealed that walking, rather than anything more dramatic, was the most frequent activity reported in dreams. This was followed by running — another basic human activity — then riding, talking, sitting,

watching, socializing, playing, manual work, quarrelling and, lastly, fighting. It is interesting that the violent activities come low on the list, while, apart from annual festivities, vacational activities are absent altogether. This may be because such activities feature most often in Level One dreams, which tend to be less memorable.

EMOTIONS

Of the emotions occurring within dreams, 64 percent were unpleasant, while only 18 percent were pleasant. This seems to contrast with the fact that the overall experience of dreaming was reported as more often pleasant than unpleasant – 41 percent as opposed to 23 percent, with the remaining dreams presumably neutral. However, this could be explained if either the pleasant emotions were experienced more strongly than the unpleasant ones, or if the mind repressed the distressing details of the latter.

Anxiety is a fact of life and, not surprisingly, was the most frequently experienced emotion in dreams. Dreams of falling, drowning, failing to catch a train or a flight, being lost or losing important items can all relate to the anxieties of waking life,

either directly or symbolically. Dreams of nameless dread or hidden menace are usually Level Two dreams, and often they can be traced back to childhood fears.

It is no surprise that anger at all such tribulations, as well as at the perceived injustices of life and the unacceptable actions of others, is the second most common emotion in dreams. Happiness and excitement come next, sometimes reflecting the innocent optimism of childhood. Such positive dreams are potent reminders that we carry the potential for joy and exuberance throughout life. Last on the list comes sadness, one of life's deepest and most affecting emotions.

In some cases, of course, dreams are emotionally neutral, yet this does not mean they are less interesting. Like all dreams, these are full of symbols and meaning, and just as important to interpret. Neutral dreams may simply suggest that the dreamer is well-balanced emotionally and not given to extremes. For some, the value of dreams may be largely that they provide escape from daily life, into a dimension where one can enjoy just being, instead of striving and doing.

Dream Workshop No. 3

The Dreamer

Juliet, a 32-year-old lawyer, is engaged to be married to her partner of five years. Her parents split acrimoniously when she was 11, an event that she feels still strongly affects her daily life and that of her sister.

THE DREAM

Juliet finds herself in an elevator in the inside of a small but cavernous cathedral, where she experiences strong feelings of familiarity and melancholy. She looks for the buttons to press to get to the top floor where she has arranged to meet her fiancé and their (in reality as yet unborn) child for dinner. Reaching for the right number, Juliet finds that all the buttons have become detached. Suddenly, the elevator is moving and, on each passing floor, through a window in the door Juliet observes chairs, vases and other objects from her childhood home. Abruptly, she finds herself in a bedroom halfway up the cathedral, which is at once strange yet familiar. Her younger sister is sitting in the middle of the room, knitting pairs of gloves, which she adds to a pile. She urges Juliet to join in the task. Panicking that she will be late for dinner and feeling sadness because the elevator has disappeared, Juliet tries to alert her sister to her distress but, much to her frustration, finds herself unable to speak.

THE INTERPRETATION

The juxtaposition of a modern **Elevator** with an ancient, sacred **Cathedral** is striking, and suggests a strong sense of movement in Juliet's inner life – possibly connnected with the idea of impending marriage and motherhood, as well as the unhappy domestic past that she is leaving behind. Failing to find the right **Elevator Button** is a typical symbol of anxiety about the future, reasonable enough in view of the major life changes awaiting her.

The **Furniture** glimpsed through the elevator doors is a further nostalgic reminder of the life history that has gone to make Juliet who she is. The part-strange, part-familiar bedroom where the lift stops might represent the meeting of future and past, while her sister's **Knitting** is perhaps symbolic of becoming knotted in the past – an urge that Juliet fears in herself.

Gloves are often interpreted as symbols of closeness ("hand in glove"), sometimes of a sexual nature (the close union of two bodies), and the invitation to join her sister in glove-making may be an attempt to reassure her that all will be well. Nevertheless, Juliet's sadness persists, caused both by regret for lost opportunities for happiness in the past and by the fear that she may not meet the expectations of her future husband and child.

Finding herself **Unable to Speak** to her sister is another common feature of an anxiety dream, suggesting emotional isolation. To avoid being alone with our life history and our memories, it is crucial to make connections. Juliet must ensure that her past does not smother her hopes for happiness.

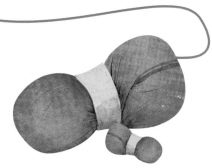

*W*hen family members appear in a dream, this may be a clue that the meaning is rooted in the past. If sadness and panic are the pervasive emotions, it is likely that deep–seated family issues are involved. Anxiety dreams of this kind seldom offer solutions — except to underline the importance of outgrowing the past and living in the present.

Common Dream Types

While our dreams may vary widely in their details, drawing their material from our individual experiences of life, we all tend to experience similar types of dreams. Those that contain strong themes and emotions can be particularly revealing.

REPETITIONS AND PATTERNS

Recurring dreams or those with recurring themes present us with issues that the unconscious recognizes as particularly important. Usually associated with the personal unconscious and occasionally with the collective unconscious, they serve either to bring unacknowledged concerns to our attention or to reflect enduringly important aspects of ourselves. Recurring dreams often provoke anxiety and usually cease when the underlying problems have been identified and addressed. Dreams featuring recurring themes are usually more pleasant, and tend to return over the years, as if giving the dreamer feedback on current life circumstances, using their variations in an attempt to clarify and modify the dream message. Both types provide valuable insights into unconscious fears or conflicts and into possible changes of direction in the inner or outer life.

SEXUAL DREAMS

Sigmund Freud considered our dream adventures to be primarily **an acting out of the sexual and the aggressive urges** present in human nature. As these urges are repressed by our social training, they are able to express themselves only in the symbols and disguises of our dreams. Most dream experts now recognize that dreams are much more than sexual wish-fulfilment. Nevertheless, sex is certainly a frequently recurring theme. One survey published some years ago found that 85 percent of men and 72 percent of women reported having sexual dreams, a finding that challenges Freud's argument that such dreams tend to be disguised to avoid prompting the censorship of the conscious mind. But what do we mean by sexual dreams? If we mean only those dreams that are sexually arousing, the percentages defined as "sexual" by dreamers would probably be much lower. Yet, if by "sexual" we mean dreams that include sexual themes, such as nudity, caresses and sexual suggestion, though excluding intercourse, the percentages may be higher.

Freud's sexual dream theories were considered controversial in *fin-de-siècle*

Vienna, where sex would commonly have been feared as a dark mystery no one ever spoke about, but even today sex can be fraught with anxiety for many people, even those who are sexually experienced. Peer pressure — to be sexually active, to have orgasms or erections, to be experimental — can be a powerful force even in an age when individualism is valued, and it can surface in troubled dreams.

When you dream of **others watching you while you perform** the sexual **act**, this could be a reflection of peer pressure, or within an established relationship it might be connected with other adults who have an emotional stake in you of some sort — for example, parents-in-law, or a boyfriend's siblings, or even his friends. They may be people who are jealous of you, who think you are unworthy of your mate, or who worry that your attachment might be selfishly erotic rather than emotionally caring. If you can identify any such people, consider what you should do, if anything, to address their feelings. The correct response might involve discussions with your partner rather than giving any signal explicitly to the onlookers. Remember that other people's feelings are not necessarily your responsibility, and if someone is anxious that you have entered a sexual or emotional relationship, that could well be their problem rather than yours.

Often in dreams we reveal inappropriate desires — perhaps for our teacher, our doctor, our plumber, our tenant, or for a teenager who is studying with our son or daughter. We may, of course, unconsciously wish to have intercourse with them — the thought might have flashed across our minds, and if so, it is likely that the unconscious would store such a moment in its memory, whereas our conscious impulse would no doubt be to brush the thought aside, into that inner trash can to which we assign the unthinkable.

Another possibility is that we are drawn to this person for some special quality they have — perhaps something missing from our own psychological make-up or from that of our partner. It might even be a kind of envy that manifests itself not as a dislike of the person, but **as wanting *to be* them**. The unconscious may mischievously convert this feeling into sexual attraction, whereas in fact it is simply pyschic attraction.

More explicitly sexual dreams can be a way of indicating sexual tensions or frustrations, but deeper meanings may also arise during

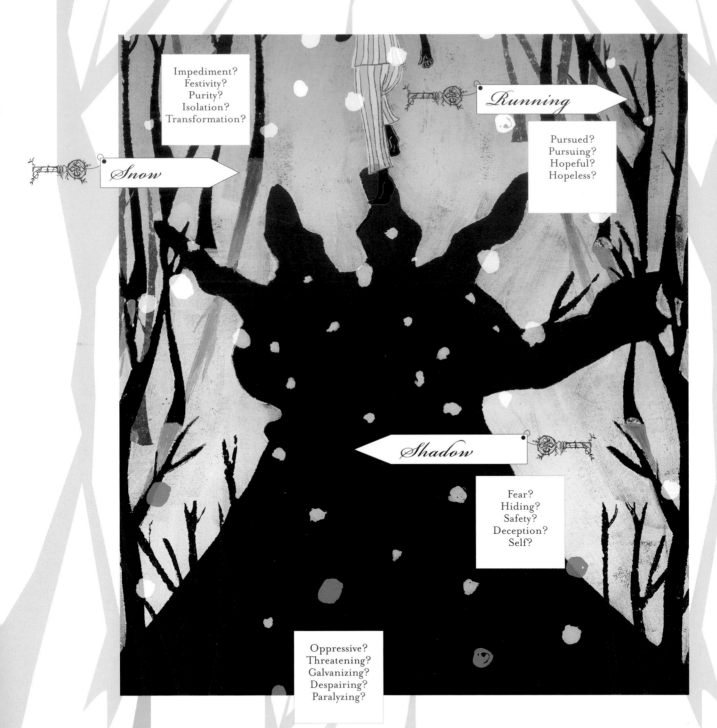

Impediment?
Festivity?
Purity?
Isolation?
Transformation?

Running

Pursued?
Pursuing?
Hopeful?
Hopeless?

Snow

Shadow

Fear?
Hiding?
Safety?
Deception?
Self?

Oppressive?
Threatening?
Galvanizing?
Despairing?
Paralyzing?

Mood cues

interpretation. What may be revealed is a desire for union with aspects of oneself (mind with body, conscious with unconscious, extroverted side with introverted side), a wish to be a parent, a need to overcome social divisions and boundaries, or even an urge to become one with the rest of creation.

NIGHTMARES

Emotions generally help us with dream interpretation, but this is not usually the case with nightmares. These dreams often prove so disturbing that more revealing emotions become submerged in terror. What tells us a great deal, however, is the *cause* of the terror. Sometimes this will be obvious: perhaps we are in danger of being shot or beaten, or injured in some other way. At other times the cause is less clear. Dread may be triggered by something seemingly innocuous like a slowly opening door, a closed box or a silent person seated with his back turned.

Studies show that people who regularly experience nightmares tend to be open and sensitive by nature. They may have a genetic predisposition to night terrors and disturbing dreams, particularly if there is no evidence that they have suffered more stressful events than normal in childhood. Nightmares that start in adult life are usually associated with life-threatening events, such as car accidents, or with ego-threatening experiences, such as important interviews or examinations. They tend to relive the events concerned, as if the unconscious needs to keep repeating them until they have been fully accepted and laid to rest by the conscious mind.

But why does a dream need to turn itself into a nightmare? It may simply be that the unconscious is unaware of the emotional impact such dreams have. When the conscious mind becomes aware of our distress, it often arouses us from sleep. Another reason might be that this is the easiest way of making a dream memorable. Nightmares are rarely forgotten the following morning.

The lack of intention to produce terror is apparent from the fact that if we can learn to face up to the source of the fear while dreaming (for example, by turning to confront a nameless menace), then it immediately becomes harmless or disappears. Moreover, once the meaning of a nightmare has been identified, frequently it does not recur to distress us.

Dream Workshop No. 4

The Dreamer

Jessica, a nine-year-old schoolgirl and a gifted pupil, has suffered a loss of self-esteem and confidence after being bullied by two girls, Desiree and Lisa, who were previously her best friends.

THE DREAM

Jessica is in her classroom at school when her teacher tells everyone to line up in an orderly fashion and then go outside because "the dragon is coming". There is an atmosphere of urgency, but not of panic. The children form a line and then march to the playground. Despite having rushed to the front of the line, Jessica finds herself inexplicably at the back. Desiree and Lisa, now at the front, look back at her and laugh. But soon she is standing in the playground with everyone else. She sees fire and smoke billowing from the school and can hear the dragon roaring. Suddenly, a car pulls up outside the school. Jessica knows it has come to rescue her, and she gets in, eager to escape. As the car sets off, she waves to all her classmates through the rear window, but none of them waves back.

INTERPRETATION

Not surprisingly, Jessica's dream is set in a **School**, not only because this is where children meet and work with each other but also because for children of her age it can be the source of a whole range of anxieties.

The **Dragon**, a powerful symbol for children, is anxiety personified. It enters the school, rendering the classroom a place of fear to which Jessica cannot return.

Her desire to escape is symbolized by the **Car** that comes to rescue her — all the more potent as a symbol if a car normally takes her home. Driving off in the car separates her from her schoolmates, who do not return Jessica's **Wave** — perhaps she feels friendless because no one in her class is actively helping her to fend off the bullies, or perhaps she feels that everyone dislikes her for standing out as a victim.

Jessica's position initially at the **Front** and then at the **Back of the Line** demonstrates the uncertainty of childhood. Things change rapidly: one moment a child can be popular, the next, unpopular. Friendships are crucial for children, influencing the way they see themselves and their emotional lives. The fact that Jessica's **Former Friends** replace her at the front of the line shows the dominance they have over her feelings.

Children who are bullied suffer deeply and can often be marked for life as a result, while the sadism enjoyed by bullies hampers their own development as well. There is little that a sensitive nine-year-old child can do to change her attitude toward being bullied. A parent could tell her that, by showing her distress, she only gives the bullies the gratification they seek, and that ignoring them would be the best policy; but this is much easier said than done. Jessica needs extra love at this difficult time, and enjoying a happy period with her parents before bedtime may help to ease her fears and prevent them from entering into her sleep. If they have not already done so, her parents must also draw the school's attention to the bullying.

*I*mages of real or imaginary animals feature frequently in children's dreams, reflecting, of course, their importance in the books children read. Do not assume that a creature such as a dragon is merely a whimsical entertainment. In a dream, however fascinated your child is by its fictional embodiments, it can appear as an intense symbol of anxiety.

Methods of Interpretation

Dream interpretation is more of an art than a science. We can never be dogmatic about the meaning of a dream, for we have to take account of the dreamer's circumstances and life history, as well as the events the dream depicts. The emotional tone of the dream and its impact upon the dreamer are also important. This is why dream dictionaries that give standard meanings for symbols can be misleading: unless an interpretation strikes a chord with you, there is a fair chance that it isn't right.

Many of the most helpful guidelines for interpretation derive from the work of Freud and Carl Jung (see pp.19-20), both of whom recognized that some of the common themes running through the great myths and legends of the world also appear in dreams. Such themes originate in the deep levels of the unconscious and reveal the major psychological, moral and romantic concerns of the human race. Freud, Jung and others also studied the way that dreams could illuminate a client's state of mind during psychotherapy, when meaning was allowed to arise spontaneously. This showed the extent to which even some modern objects have come to take on typical symbolic meanings.

Motor cars frequently suggest travel, power and sexuality for many dreamers, as well as fear and risk for those who have been involved in car accidents.

Calvin Hall's research into common dream themes (see pp.38-39) illustrates the role of straightforward inquisition in dream interpretation. To use the earlier example of a house as a dream image of the self, you need to examine the image in detail. What emotions are associated with each of the rooms? Is the house a happy place, or does it feel cold and menacing? Is it tidy or cluttered, open to the outside world or enclosed and secret?

Both Freud and Jung developed methods for assisting dream interpretation that depend upon association — the way in which one word, or the object or picture it describes, suggests others and ultimately leads to a word that is key to the dream's meaning. Freud considered the possibility that dreams use this symbolic language because their true meaning may be so disturbing, exciting or revealing that the conscious mind would be aroused from sleep. An alternative explanation is that the dream uses, in an opportunistic way, any available images that fit the story it is weaving, leaving it to the dreamer to tease

out the underlying meaning. Whatever the truth may be, working upon the associations that are suggested to you by individual images can often help to encourage meaning to emerge. Both free association and word association work particularly well if the starting point is a geometrical symbol or an archetypal figure, as they can potentially unlock the richest chain of associations. We should always look carefully to see if these things feature in our dreams anywhere.

FREE ASSOCIATION

Developed by Freud, free association works by allowing the mind to start with the dream image and then to spin off a string of associations, each suggested by the one that precedes it. Thus a dream image of a book might be followed by the association *reading*, which might be followed by *ideas*, then by a chain of associations, such as *adventure*, *mountains*, *climbing*, *pathway*, *monastery*, *bell*, *prayer*, *worship*, *spirit* and finally *the Divine*. At this point the dreamer realizes that the words *the Divine* in fact carry special impact, and prompt her to acknowledge that she has long been experiencing spiritual anxiety, from which she has tried to hide in books and abstract ideas. Now that she has made this acknowledgment, the dreamer is able to identify that her spiritual anxiety derives from a deep-seated sense of sin and personal worthlessness. This in turn suggests that she should focus less on the intellectual side of her life and more on the need to heal her damaged emotional side.

Just like any method of dream interpretation, free association is far from infallible. Nevertheless, it is a good way to uncover hidden unconscious material. The method can be tried more than once with the same image, but if none of the associations prompts a powerful sense of recognition, it is time to begin work on another image from the dream or wait until further dreams provide more information.

DIRECT ASSOCIATION

Jung believed that the drawback of free association is that it can take the dreamer too far from the dream. It might well uncover important insights into the unconscious, but these insights may not necessarily be the ones the dream seeks to convey. Jung preferred a method known as direct word association, in which instead of allowing one association to suggest another, you return each time to the image. It helps to write the dream image in the middle of a sheet of paper and note all the associations in a circle around it. If we use the book example again, word association might produce the following results:

life

pages   *pleasure*

study

success   *words*

stories   *characters*

achievement

satisfaction   *inspiration*

ending

plot   *ideas*

This method gives the dreamer a better chance of exploring all the associations to an image, and considering them as a whole. After studying the group in the above example, the dreamer might confess that he has always had a secret ambition to become an author, but fear of rejection has prevented him from trying to make the ambition a reality. The dream reminds him that creativity is a hugely important part of his nature.

DREAM DIALOGUES

Another method of dream interpretation is to carry out a dialogue with the characters or objects in the dream. Frequently they will represent aspects of yourself, and an imaginary conversation with them can help to clarify their meaning.

Sit quietly with your eyes closed and visualize the dream person, object or animal you wish to speak with, then ask them what they would like to tell you. Don't attempt to "create" their answers: allow them to arise spontaneously. If you wish the character or object to leave you alone, tell it so. If you wish to see it again, invite it to return. Try changing places with it and imagine that it is speaking through you. At the end of the talk, gently dissolve the visualization, open your eyes and ponder what has been said.

This method is, however, less suitable if the person you dream about is known to you in waking life and you feel that the dream character represents themselves rather than archetypal figures or aspects of yourself. You may project your own bias into what they say, and mislead yourself in consequence. In this instance, it is better simply to ask yourself *why* you are dreaming about that person. Are there unresolved issues between you both? If so, is there some way in which you might be able to resolve them?

DREAM CONTINUATION

Many dreams seem to end prematurely, leaving the feeling that we have been deprived of an important conclusion. By visualizing the dream up to the point where it ended, it is sometimes possible to re-enter it and allow it to continue. Don't treat the results as seriously as you would a real dream. There is always a risk that they may not be accurate. And be careful that the conscious mind does not try to take over and tailor the ending to its own wishes. Try to let your mind drift back into the dream and contact the level of unconscious from which it arose.

REMAINING CONSCIOUS DURING DREAMING

Eastern spiritual traditions teach that we go through our lives half-asleep to the nature of reality. Many of their practices are designed to make us more attentive to experience, and to break the habits and conditioning that obscure our perception. If we are inattentive while awake, we are even more inattentive while asleep. We ignore the fact that dreams are as important to the development of our consciousness as the waking state.

Different methods for remaining conscious during dreaming are described later in this book (see p.160-163), but one preliminary exercise is to ask yourself how you know you are not dreaming right now. What clues tell you that you are awake? What can you observe? Try this reality check several times each day.

ATTENTION TO DETAIL

When interpreting dreams, the more detail we have, the better. Keep the following questions in mind:

Why did I dream about that? Even in Level One dreams that deal with familiar, preconscious material, there has still been a selection process at work. What details did the dream select and why?

What emotions did the dream events cause, and why? Dreams often treat emotions as illogically as they treat events. A dreamer may be unmoved when witnessing a scene that in waking life would be disturbing, or upset by something that normally would seem trivial. Illogical emotional responses can indicate that scenes are symbolic — though the emotions *can* give clues about the issues being symbolized.

Are there any particularly unreal objects in the dream? Usually, dream objects are similar to objects in real life, but when they appear or behave in unexpected ways — animals that talk, stairs that lead nowhere, knives that won't cut — they may carry particularly strong symbolic meaning.

Are the colours natural or unnatural? The colours in dreams can be particularly vivid, particularly muted, or relatively normal. There may be a preponderance of certain hues and an absence of others. Such anomalous features can be important in the search for meanings.

What about the scenery? The setting may be breathtakingly beautiful or grey and drab, menacing or comforting, urban or rural, indoors or outside, restful or arousing, and so on. Ask yourself why the dream might have had that location and mood.

What clothes are you wearing? Generally, dreamers are unaware of their clothing, and miss a rich vein of possible symbolism. Clothes can symbolize how we wish the world to see us, or represent aspects of who we are, or think we are. Tell yourself during the day that you will look down at yourself or in a mirror the next time you dream.

Whom do you meet? Some people dream mostly of strangers, not loved ones. This may indicate the absence of hidden conflicts or insecurities in relationships. Strangers may symbolize aspects of ourselves or of the way we experience the world. Look for patterns. Are they more often of one sex? Friendly or hostile? Talkative or silent? Helpful or unhelpful?

DIFFICULTIES IN INTERPRETATION

Some people worry that dream interpretation may tell them things about themselves that they would rather not know. Others complain that their dreams are so nonsensical that they defy interpretation. Others worry if their interpretations are likely to be correct.

Except perhaps for those from Level Three, dreams are not omniscient. The unaided human mind is never infallible. And although dreams are revealing, they do make mistakes — overemphasizing some things, underemphasizing some, and perhaps neglecting others entirely. Fundamentally, dreams are always trying to be helpful, even though, rather like well-meaning people, they may go about it in the wrong way. They "intend" to bring to your notice issues within your control in ways from which you will benefit. If you would prefer not to know these things, that may be because you fear change.

As for nonsensical dreams, it is true that some dreams are so bizarre and confused that it is difficult even to know where to start. The best approach is to look for any recurrent themes rather than to treat each dream as a whole. If using free or direct association, you may have to form a range of responses, until one is found that resonates particularly strongly and points to the hidden meaning. However, unless significant factors can be identified, it is best not to work too hard on apparently nonsensical dreams, but spend time on those that are more coherent. Dream interpretation is a lengthy process, and although no time spent on interpretation is ever really wasted, some dreams repay effort more than others.

Appreciate as well that just like dreams themselves, dream interpretation is not infallible. Look upon it as providing hints and whispers rather than certainty. If any interpretation doesn't feel right, the chances are that it probably isn't. Interpretations won't necessarily feel comfortable, but they should always be broadly compatible with what you know about yourself.

People sometimes ask whether two similar dreams can ever have different meanings. Providing that the first interpretation identified the significant features of the dream and proved acceptable to the dreamer, the second dream may have a different meaning. If dreams are satisfactorily interpreted, they are rarely repeated.

Dream Workshop No. 5

The Dreamer

Keith, 32, is doing well in his work as a freelance yoga teacher. His current clients are loyal, enthusiastic and generous, so he feels valued and confident. But he worries that he might be putting all his eggs in one basket, as he is so busy concentrating on the moment that he hasn't made any concrete plans for the future.

THE DREAM

Keith sees a large wooden doorway with a flashing sign above it saying "Hello". He wonders what's behind it and decides to go through, his heart racing with excitement and fear. He finds himself in a small room. The only way out seems to be the door through which he came in. But in front of him is a huge red velvet curtain.

His cell phone rings, but when he answers it there is no one there. Instead, a hand appears from behind the curtain, wearing a satin glove and presenting a golden key. The phone rings again and another hand appears, this time wearing a white shirt with smart cufflinks and holding a scroll. Keith shouts out, "Who are you? Who's there?" But there's no reply. A third hand appears; this time a bare arm is presenting a plate of delicious-looking fruit. Keith feels as though someone is watching over him and doesn't know what to do. He thinks one of the items might give him access to the other side of the curtain, but which one? Maybe he should turn back the way he came? He turns round, but the door has disappeared. In its place is a window looking out onto a bright landscape of rolling hills, one of which has on top of it a cherry tree in blossom.

INTERPRETATION

Although **Doors** can symbolize both entrances and exits, in this case the likely interpretation is new openings, new opportunities — as suggested by the large, welcoming sign above. However, the **Room** Keith enters is small. This might imply that he sees only limited possibilities.

In the enigmatic way of dreams, Keith then sees a large **Red Velvet Curtain**, which implies that the room is much bigger than he thought. A curtain also suggests theatre and make-believe. Perhaps the new opportunities in Keith's life are simply an illusion.

We then have the problem of the **Three Hands**. Their appearance may suggest that there are, in fact, definite possibilities. The first hand, with the **Satin Glove and Golden Key**, seems to suggest financial success. The second, with the **White Shirt and Scroll**, appears to represent a professional life. The third, with the **Bare Arm and the Fruit**, seems to denote health and healing, with relative poverty but personal satisfaction and seeds for the future. Another option is suggested by the bright landscape behind the dreamer. If he stays with his present way of life, there is still the possibility of fruit (fruition), symbolized by the cherry blossom.

Is Keith being told that he should not be deceived by apparent opportunities, or is he being shown that these opportunities are genuinely open to him? With the ring of his **Cell Phone**, Keith might expect to receive more information. However, no one responds. Keith isn't going to get the answers he is seeking from anyone other than from himself.

A dream will not usually make clear whether a symbol held out like a gift is genuine or illusory
— and when the setting has such a character of theatricality, one must beware of false friends.
Here the dreamer is presented with an allegory of choice, as in a Grail legend or fairy story.
Only Keith can tell whether these offers are genuine solutions or dangerous temptations.

Problem Solving & Healing

We have seen how interpretation can yield quite complex analyses of dreams, often with many ambiguities. We might find ourselves tracing threads of meaning over a sequence of dreams, for weeks or longer. This is a gradual self-revelation, and can help us to understand and begin to resolve some of our issues. But it can also be revealing to actually submit a problem to the dreaming mind. The idea is to go to bed in a spirit of enquiry. This can be formalized, in the manner of ancient traditions. You might meditate in candlelight – perhaps focusing mentally on the candle. Then you might speak a question to your unconscious mind, humbly asking it to give you the privilege of an overnight answer.

Next morning, on awakening, search your dream for the answer to your question. The connection between the dream's symbolism and your problem may be elusive, in which case proceed by hypothesis: if the dream were telling you how to give a speech next week without being tongue-tied by nerves, what would it be conveying? The procedure is rather like using the Tarot: the significance might need to be teased out of cryptic imagery by the innate wisdom of your unconscious.

A good place to start work of this kind is with a problem to which there is an objective solution – like an anagram. Hold the puzzle in your mind as you fall asleep, telling yourself that your dreams will find the answer. Review your dream memories in the morning – the answer may be presented symbolically.

Recent research has shown that with exercises such as this, we can actually improve the neurological connections in the brain, boosting our memory and keeping the mind active as we age. So not only do dreams provide psychological healing by assisting us with emotional problems, they may also contribute to physical well-being.

Physical health problems require proper medical care, but dreams can help to foster healing by drawing on the power of the unconscious. If we have back trouble, for example, we may get into the habit of thinking that we have a "bad" back. Simply telling ourselves during the day, and before sleep, that we have a "good" back that can heal itself is of great value. If each night we visualize ourselves moving freely, without pain, this image starts to enter our dreams, reinforcing the message to our body that healing is what we want – and know we can achieve.

Visualization

Improving visualization skills can extend your ability to control your dreams. We have seen how paying close attention to the moment (see p. 37) can help to enrich your dream life, and you can develop this aptitude by encouraging yourself to not only be aware of the different environments that you pass through in waking life, but to really look at them and attend to the details. What lies beyond your immediate foreground? How does the play of light affect what you see? Patterns, light, tints, textures and shapes surround us wherever we go, so try to actively take notice of these phenomena. Notice the people you encounter — what they look like, what they are doing, what they are wearing. Improving your observational skills will probably start to make your dreams more memorable, and when trying to recapture the precise appearance of the symbolic objects that crop up in your dreams, you will be more likely to have success.

Try out modest exercises during the day to fix your mind on the objects around you. Focus on something in front of you — perhaps a banana you are about to have for breakfast. Look carefully at all its features — texture, colour, shape, markings. Now close your eyes, holding the image of the banana in your mind. Mentally change its hue, then return it back to normal. Imagine that the banana is starting to rot, and watch its skin blacken. Reverse the process, so the banana freshens, returning to being a delicious fruit. Open your eyes and see how closely your imagined banana resembles the real one in front of you. You can try this with anything, even a person, altering their appearance until they have changed into something totally different. In dreams, objects or people will often transform themselves without any warning. Honing your visualization skills will help you to become aware of this as it happens and to notice the significance of those changes.

Dream Workshop No. 6

The Dreamer
Horace, 60, is a jazz musician who plays the saxophone. He has been married three times and has five children and seven grandchildren. His current wife has just been given a clean bill of health after having had a life-saving operation.

THE DREAM

Horace is visiting the hospital where his wife was a patient. He is due to play in a concert there, but when he opens his instrument case, he finds his saxophone has turned into a trumpet, an instrument he can't play very well. The scene then changes and he is in a room with a newborn baby and an enchanting little girl. The girl looks up at him, smiles sweetly and points to a corner. "Can you see the wicked witch hiding under the chair?" she asks. He glances beneath the chair but sees nothing. He shakes his head in reply and notices for the first time that the little girl has wings, like an angel. Then the baby starts to cry. Horace feels at a loss, as he doesn't know what to do to comfort it.

INTERPRETATION

It is natural that Horace's dreams may relive, in symbolic form, some of the memories relating to his wife's illness, which probably placed great strain on him. The fact that he is due to play in a **Concert** at the hospital probably represents his recollection that he has had to put on a "performance" of optimism and cheerfulness when visiting his wife, and his sense of inadequacy or discomfort at doing so may be symbolized by the fact that

he will instead have to play a **Trumpet**, an instrument on which he is not proficient, rather than his saxophone.

The dream then changes with the introduction of the newborn **Baby** and the **Little Girl**. Horace has five children, and it is understandable that he may also associate hospitals with childbirth. However, the little girl is more difficult to interpret, and Horace could benefit from working on this symbolism. There may be something of the archetypal Divine Child about the girl, in which case she symbolizes innocence, purity and natural wisdom. Her wings certainly add to this possibility. If this is the case, she and the baby may represent new beginnings, and may be warning him not to allow the **Witch** (damaging aspects of his own nature perhaps?) to intrude and spoil things. The baby bursting into tears may indicate that if he does allow the "witch" to intrude into these new beginnings, everything will "end in tears".

The dream ends with Horace's **Feelings of Helplessness** as he is unable to decide how to comfort the baby. This image may simply stem from his understandable feelings of inadequacy while his wife was ill. But now that she is out of hospital, he should try not to dwell on these negative thoughts. Horace needs to focus on his gratitude that she is well again, and on the various practical things he is able to do for her now and in the future.

WAA!

Archetypes in a dream need to be interpreted with care, as sometimes they have additional meanings. The witch here may suggest the dark side of the Mother, personifying the illness that attacked Horace's wife and threatened to remove her loving support. However, it could also be an aspect of Horace's own destructiveness if he allows his anxieties free rein.

3

Guide to Dream Symbols

Symbols are more ancient than words, and, rather like music, they have the power to touch us directly, deep in our core. In dreams they can carry profound meanings, often multiple ones. They can startle us, haunt us or elevate our spirits. They form some of the building blocks of the unconscious. Here we take a look at some of the common types of dream symbols, and provide guidance on their interpretation.

Introduction to Dream Symbols

Sigmund Freud, as we have seen, believed that dreams use symbols to disguise meanings that might be so disturbing, if presented directly, that they would arouse the conscious mind. Carl Jung argued that symbols are simply the *language* of the unconscious. This seems closer to the truth.

Symbols are all around us, every day. Advertisers use them to associate products with happiness, relaxation, wealth, beauty or sexual success, though true symbols arise from the unconscious rather than from the conscious mind. A major characteristic of the human mind is our readiness to let one thing stand for another.

Dream symbols often operate in the same way as metaphor, which we use all the time – in conversation, in letters or emails, in our conscious thinking, and in our creative endeavours. Increasingly people refer to the learning process as a "journey". The word has several related connotations, implying that we are making progress in a long-term project, that it is a highly individual experience, and that we end up in a very different place from where we started. The metaphor of the journey often occurs in dreams, and tends to have similar associations.

Metaphor is the stock-in-trade of dreaming, and you do not have to be a poet to be able to appreciate its layers of meaning. These may be multiple. A clock obviously suggests time, but perhaps it has other connotations, too: if it has a round face, this might imply symmetry or perfection; if it ticks loudly, this might indicate irritating repetition. Time, in any case, can be friend or foe: it can evoke different emotions, depending on whether we face a weekend unaccustomedly alone or are racing to meet a deadline. Personal factors may be operating: if the clock is an heirloom, this might allude to your relationship with a parent or other relative, perhaps a deceased one.

Many dream symbols are easy to interpret, but even when their meaning seems obvious, there may also be a deeper significance hidden beneath it. For example, if I dream of being locked out of my house, the most plausible interpretation is that I am anxious and insecure about something – perhaps I can guess that this relates to worries about my job performance, or fractures in my marriage. However, if I want to be more precise about my anxiety, I need to work on the specific symbolism of the key. Keys are

for opening or unlocking something, so what is it that I am anxious to unlock? Is it something I have failed to understand about my partner's emotional responses? Is it a mutually supportive social network that I feel excluded from at work? Is it a skill that would benefit me — perhaps emotional intelligence, or computer or leadership skills? Further investigation of the possibilities may provide the answer.

In studying your dreams, you will notice that certain symbols recur, and/or that some symbols carry a strong emotional charge. These are the ones that will yield the richest insights in a session of interpretation. If free or direct association (see pp. 49-50) does not reveal their meaning, hold them lightly in your mind over the following days. Play with them mentally from time to time, as if they represent an intriguing puzzle. If the meaning still does not arise, ask your unconscious to work on it for you. Use a simple, direct request such as, "Please find the meaning of … for me." Then put the puzzle out of your conscious mind for a while, giving the unconscious time to incubate it. The answer will often come to you out of the blue when you least expect it.

Dream symbols are not deliberately intended to be obscure. Like musical notation, they can be read more easily with practice. Even so, dreams sometimes seem to get carried away by their own creative powers. Like storytellers who lose the thread, they can go off at a tangent, as if one symbol suggests another, which then suggests another and so on … until the dream becomes increasingly confused. When this happens, recognize that you are working on several dreams in one, and try to separate out the themes before interpreting each one individually. In the process of doing this, you may see how they are connected, which can sometimes reveal another level of meaning.

It is an interesting exercise to ask what we ourselves symbolize, both in waking life and in dreams. Some dreamers feel they are the onlooker, always aware of what is happening but never a part of it. Others may see themselves as a seeker, a victim, a helper or a leader. The majority see that they have different functions at different times, just as Shakespeare reminds us that each man in his life plays many parts. It is always worth asking what we can learn about ourselves from our symbolic dream roles.

Dream Workshop No. 7

The Dreamer

Alan, 25, is a soldier who has been on active service in some of the world's troublespots. Despite the risks, he loves his job and relishes the camaraderie of army life. A gregarious and witty man who is popular with his comrades, he also has a sensitive side.

THE DREAM

Alan and his best friend John are on leave. They are about to return to their hotel after a night out when Alan bets John that he can beat him there in a race. They set off running together until Alan takes a shortcut down an alley. Suddenly, he finds himself in a maze. He knows that he has to find his way out, but whichever way he goes he seems to reach a dead end. Annoyed, he climbs up onto a tree stump to try to find the exit. To his surprise there is a radiant star not far above his head, and he stretches up to grab it. The star glows in his hand and he somehow knows that it will guide him out of the maze.

INTERPRETATION

Comradeship is essential to army life, so it is no surprise that Alan's **Best Friend** appears in his dream. A friend often symbolizes good times, sharing both emotional and physical safety. **Betting** is also a common pastime for young soldiers, but is there more to it than just this?

Hotels are impersonal, transitory places, so staying with a friend would seem preferable to being there alone. Why does Alan think that returning first is worth the separation and the physical effort involved?

A **Shortcut** can reveal a desire to make things easy for ourselves, and even a willingness to take an unfair advantage. But Alan discovers that this shortcut leads to a **Maze**, often a place of confusion and anxiety. This ominous outcome may represent the soldier's vulnerability when separated from comrades during conflict. However, there is another, very different possibility. Mazes are traditional symbols of religion, representing humankind's search for the way back to the source, or to the Divine. Once in the maze, the seeker must frequently retrace his or her steps in order to find the correct route. Might Alan be questioning the moral worth of his job?

Much of the meaning of this dream depends on what the **Star** represents to Alan. It may extend the religious imagery, suggesting that spirituality can guide him, and help him to make sense of the confusing demands of being a soldier. Alternatively, a star may well carry military significance for him, standing for the insignia of an officer's rank or for campaign medals. A soldier must obey orders, and the star's positive attributes here may suggest that Alan has faith in his superiors to lead him well. Another possibility is that it reveals his personal ambition. Racing back to the hotel would then appear to show competitive spirit, so the maze might be a warning that Alan's competitiveness may lead to trouble, especially if it separates him from his comrades. Only Alan can decide the right interpretation, considering the associations of all these symbols.

Certain universal symbols, like the star, are so potent that they have
        everyday manifestations in various walks of life. Alan's star could be a military medal
(personal ambition?) or a badge of authority (sense of duty?), but it might also indicate
        spiritual aspirations. Interpretation needs to unravel such ambiguities.

People

O f all the images that feature in dreams, people are potentially the most intriguing. They may represent themselves, other people, the dreamer, or **sometimes even abstract** ideas.

You may find that people seem highly significant in your dreams, or they may seem to be peripheral. Factors like these can give insights into your relationships with people in waking life. If people are remote in dreams, perhaps you could do more to benefit from relationships in daily life. On the other hand, if you are overdependent on others in dreams, perhaps you would do well to be more self-sufficient in real life. (Dreams on the whole tend to show the symptom, not the remedy — but there are plenty of exceptions to this, as we shall see.)

If your dreams predominantly feature family and friends, they may be telling you something important about your closest relationships. However, as with other details, dreams might alter a person's appearance. Sometimes the alterations may seem significant, but more usually the dream is arbitrary in such matters.

A stranger may represent an aspect of someone you know, or may point to aspects of your relationships with people in general — friends, family and strangers alike.

If the people in your dreams are mostly of the opposite sex, this may reflect your circle of friends — real or desired. But at a deeper level, **it can indicate the opposite side** of yourself. To varying degrees, we all have the qualities usually associated with both sexes — the intuitive, gentle aspects of the female and the active, courageous aspects of the male. Jung saw these as archetypal forces and named them the Anima (female side of the male) and Animus (male side of the female), as we have seen. Balancing these forces within ourselves plays an important part in maintaining psychological health.

The Anima and the Animus can also be projected outward, as the male concept of the ideal woman and the female concept of the ideal male. In Level Two dreams the Anima may be an elusive object of desire, while in Level Three she may be the enigmatic Mistress of Mysteries. Similarly, the Animus might appear as an all-powerful, all-providing adventurer in Level Two dreams, or as the Hero in Level Three. When such images occur at Level Two, they may indicate that the dreamer tends to look to the opposite

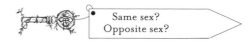

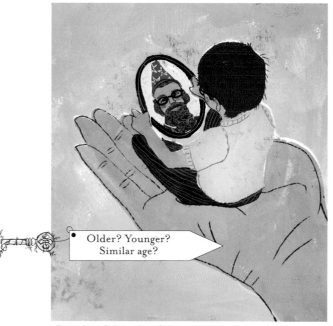

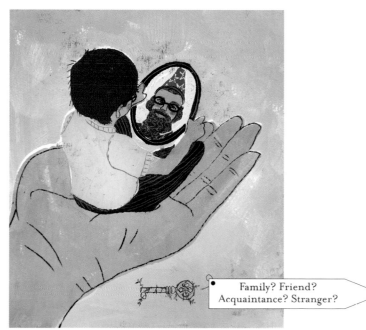

Brother? Mother? Housemate? Bank manager? Lover? Teacher? Daughter? Enemy? Colleague?

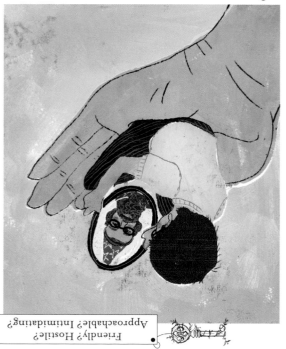

sex to supply the inner female or male qualities that he or she lacks in themselves. At Level Three these figures typically represent not only a fuller realization of such qualities but also of energies outside ourselves that assist us in our spiritual journey. So the Anima can appear in the role of the Earth Mother (fertility and sustaining love), while the Animus can be the father figure (authority and protection).

People who are younger or older than ourselves in dreams might indicate a wish to return to our youth or a fear of growing old. However, they too may be archetypes: the Divine Child (purity, innocence, intuition) and the Wise Old Man or Woman (practical wisdom, magic powers).

Even those of us who think of ourselves as solitary are in fact likely to depend on other people far more than we realize — not only for support, confidence, entertainment, understanding and so on, but also **as an ever-changing buzz of life around us.** We are all intrinsically alone within our individual consciousness, which cannot be shared or escaped. Yet we know that everyone else in the world is in exactly the same situation, which gives us kinship with them. This kinship is frequently recognized to be spiritual: we share a sacred bond. Seeing other people, even strangers, makes us aware of this bond. Dreams can provide a way for us to experience this kinship in unexpected and revealing ways.

But, of course, dreams also represent the **opposite side of the coin: the sense of another person's otherness, which may seem negative** to us. Any kind of insecurity may take human form in a dream. And it is unsurprising when in Level One dreams we meet the very people who seem to make our lives difficult during the day, and feel the same frustrations.

At Level One, dreams may seem to offer us few solutions to problems we may have with difficult people in waking life: they simply play out the issues. But by doing this they can still be of value because they offer us a prompt to ask ourselves the question: why do we *allow* ourselves to feel these emotions? Perhaps somewhere in the dream the answer to our problem lies hidden, if only we are determined enough to find it.

Level Two dreams extend the process of self-examination by helping us to see why we react as we do. They may remind us of repressed frustrations or emotional wounds from earlier in life, which we have never properly worked through. They may point to temperamental difficulties in ourselves that we have never learned how to handle. **Unspoken resentments and even jealousies may emerge** from our analysis of the dream material: by paying careful attention to the inhabitants of the dream and their (or our) symbolic actions, we may unearth a basic distrust of people, or an attempt to excuse our failures by blaming others.

By contrast, Level One and Level Two dreams can also demonstrate our love for people, our awareness of the help they render, their ability to lift our spirits and their unselfishness toward us. Such dreams recharge our emotional batteries and leave us feeling more positive about our lives. Let us say that we dream of a friend, undressing. This might seem quite shocking, but if our feelings about the friend are positive, we are simply being reminded of a good person we may have taken for granted. Undressing is not necessarily to be taken evocatively: after all, it is what we all do before going to bed.

When people of authority appear in our dreams, the feelings they excite are often strong: they reassure us by being in control or daunt us by highlighting aspects of the way we see ourselves. A company's CEO may appear in his own dream with a crown to denote superiority, or perhaps in the archetypal role of the Hero. But a sense of responsibility can also induce anxiety dreams, symbolizing any frustrations, insecurities or resentments that the dreamer may feel in waking life.

Dreaming about the dead is a classic archetypal dream, signifying resurrection. It may warn of unresolved past issues, but could also symbolize refreshing old ideas with new life. Dreams of pregnancy and giving birth may simply reflect maternal desires, but will often represent the emergence of new ideas or opportunities in the dreamer's life.

Dream Workshop No. 8

The Dreamer

Michael is a 29-year-old investment banker who is about to embark on a drastic career change: to train as an actor. He is daunted by the financial sacrifice and the uncertainty of the future, but excited by the prospect of leading a more creative life. His girlfriend, Laura, who lives with him, is supportive of his plans.

THE DREAM

Michael finds himself stepping onto a rickety wooden bridge that spans a frozen river. There are dark hills all around, unfamiliar and unwelcoming. Three women wearing nurses' uniforms are sawing up a fallen tree trunk at the far end of the bridge. As Michael walks to the middle of the bridge, he recognizes one of them as his girlfriend, Laura; the other two are strangers. The women wave to him enthusiastically, and Michael tries to run to meet Laura's embrace, but finds himself unable to reach her. He has the sensation that his legs are moving, but in fact they are not. He starts to cry and feels the tears splashing at his feet, making a puddle. The three women are crying too.

Then the sun comes out from behind a cloud, and he notices that the ice below the bridge is gradually melting. He realizes that he can now move his legs again and with great relief starts running toward the women. All around him large, luminous fish are leaping in and out of the water, high into the air. The women have disappeared, and he suddenly feels overwhelming disappointment. All the fish are staring open-mouthed in his direction, and he can hear laughter from far away.

INTERPRETATION

The **Rickety Bridge** and the **Frozen River** seem like symbols for Michael's anxiety about his new career, which will take him into unknown territory. **Laura** and the **Other Two Women** may represent his feminine side, which he will need to develop if he is to be a successful actor. The act of sawing up a fallen tree may stand for the sacrifice of his old life, while the **Nurses' Uniforms** may suggest a need for comfort and reassurance.

However, the **Weakness in his Legs** and his inability to reach his partner suggest a fear of failing her. She supports his risky career change, which involves leaving a highly-paid profession, but he may feel afraid that he will let her down. Both his own **Tears** and those of the women could represent a reversion to childhood — understandable doubts about his career move may have taken him back to his infancy, when others tended to control what happened to him.

The appearance of the **Sun,** the **Melting of the Ice** and Michael's renewed ability to run seem to provide temporary reassurance that all will be well. And the **Luminous Fish** leaping from the water could represent his creative energy being freed by his new career in the arts. But strangely, their appearance coincides with the upsetting disappearance of the three women. Is he worried about being carried away by creativity and losing touch with people? The distant laughter may be both applauding and mocking, perhaps reminding him that, in the world of the actor, tragedy and comedy can never be fully separated from each other.

*S*ometimes a dream event is unclear until you establish its underlying mood.
In this dream it's important to explore the ambiguous ending in more detail:
Is the laughter the dreamer hears a sign of ridicule or enjoyment?
If it's impossible to tell, it's best to interpret the dream in both ways to see which feels more likely.

Sexual Symbols

Just as sexual dreams can in fact be about something else entirely, so too apparently asexual dreams may have disguised erotic content. We are now in the realm of Freudian dream interpretation, **where repressed desires are censored** by the unconscious and presented to the dreaming mind as inanimate objects.

The genitalia lend themselves to a whole range of symbolic disguises. The vagina (and by extension female sexuality) would be recognized by a Freudian not only in receptacles such as purses, handbags, cups and vases but also in enclosing garments (gloves, shoes or hats) and natural phenomena such as a red rose (the colour of menstruation). A purse may also evoke the womb. Soft textures such as velvet or moss recall pubic hair. Drinking from a cup has been said to suggest oral sex with a woman. Even when Jungian overtones of the Holy Grail are identified in such a dream, there is still likely to be an element of femininity – perhaps a link with a mythic virgin cup-bearer or the archetype of the Earth Mother.

The male equipment is obviously suggested by instruments of penetration, such as knives and screwdrivers: the fact that these items are often used as weapons is consistent with the Freudian view of **the link between sex and violence.** Pencils, towers, candles, pool cues and other such phallic objects can be read in a similar way.

Other symbolic representations of sex might include anything with an appropriately rhythmic motion (say, horse riding or wood chopping) or anything that gushes explosively – such as an oil well, a burst tap or faucet, or a champagne bottle being opened. Of course, gushing water is relevant to bathtime, while the champagne bottle is relevant to a romantic evening, so both these symbols supply a suitable *context* as well as content for a dream of desire.

With just a little poetic imagination, you can extend the symbolic vocabulary of intercourse even further. Any climactic action, from the crashing of waves on the shore **to reaching a hill's summit, can be made** use of by a Freudian interpreter. However, it is important not to let the game of hunt-the-sexual-symbol overwhelm one's sensitivity to other symbols within the dream and to its mood and context.

The Body & Clothing

Dreaming of nudity is extremely common, but most frequently the dreamer is the one who is nude — it is nudity felt rather than seen. Common sense might suggest that the nudity indicates exhibitionist tendencies, but this fails to recognize the importance of the emotions experienced and the associations that emerge during subsequent interpretation. The emotion most often felt by the nude dreamer turns out to be **shame or embarrassment, especially as everyone else** in the dream is usually fully clothed, symbolizing a sense of vulnerability or a fear of self-disclosure. Yet, almost always the dreamer admits that no one else in the dream seemed to notice their nudity. The dream message says that we don't have to hide who we are, or spend our lives in a state of emotional self-protection.

Nudity is in fact one of the most potent of all symbols. Depending on the emotional responses and associations that surround it, nudity may reveal a need to express creativity, a longing for a more natural existence, or **a wish to rediscover childhood innocence** and lack of inhibition.

Explicitly sexual dreams can indicate sexual tensions, but on a deeper level may reveal a desire for union with aspects of oneself (mind with body, conscious with unconscious), a wish to be a parent, or a need to overcome social division.

Clothes both display and disguise the wearer, and their significance in dreams is often enriched by erotic associations — for example, the removal of them. Cross-dressing may indicate a rounded **personality, with masculine and feminine** sensibilities in balance; or, perhaps, a secret fascination.

The condition of the body as it is represented in a dream can reflect psychological issues that the dreamer has, or their sense of spirituality. Jung believed that bodily ailments could be reflected in a dream, and some people have even claimed that cures for illness have been similarly conveyed.

Broken teeth can signal insecurity and, like losing your hair, are a common feature of anxiety dreams. Menstruation or excretion can suggest public anxiety or a need to express the self. Spiritual health can often be symbolized through the appearance of a person's eyes, the windows of the soul. The heart is the classic symbol of emotional well-being, and a universal emblem of love.

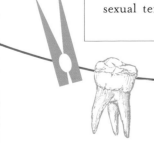

Dream Workshop No. 9

The Dreamer
Nathan, 15, is a schoolboy who is currently working toward important examinations. Over the last few weeks, he has been studying intensively with a boy and a girl from his class. He finds himself strongly attracted to the girl, but he fears that she prefers the other boy to him.

THE DREAM

Nathan is wandering around a huge mansion, stopping to look at and trying to identify the many statues and paintings. He is surprised to see on the wall a small portrait of the boy he has been studying with. Suddenly, his female classmate appears and apologizes for having kept him waiting. She ushers him over to a barber's chair and puts a towel around his neck. Then she takes out a pair of scissors from a cupboard and starts to cut his hair, which is quite long. When she has finished, she seems very pleased with the result and asks him what he thinks. But, try as he might, Nathan can't see himself clearly in the mirror: although he can see a reflection of sorts, the image is too blurred and restless to give him a good view. This makes him feel anxious, as he is keen to see his new hairstyle and hopes to compliment the girl on her handiwork.

INTERPRETATION

Houses and other buildings often emerge as symbols of ourselves, and the huge mansion in which Nathan finds himself may represent his as yet unrealized potential as a young adult. The **Statues** and **Paintings** might suggest his possible future accomplishments. He makes an effort to identify these works of art, but he does not yet fully understand them or his own potential.

The fact that Nathan sees his young rival in the form of a **Portrait** implies that he has a rather static view of him — perhaps because he has labelled him as a rival for the girl's affections rather than as a personality with feelings and ideas of his own. This attitude is unfair to the other boy. Significantly, the portrait is a "small" one, which gives the impression that Nathan is attempting to diminish his rival in his own eyes and would also like to do so in the eyes of the girl.

It is particularly interesting that when the girl appears, she at once begins to cut Nathan's **Hair**. In dreams hair is an important symbol of masculinity or femininity, and ultimately of identity. The story of Samson, who lost his strength when Delilah cut his hair, exemplifies this. In the dream the suggestion is that Nathan is surrendering power to the young girl as a consequence of his feelings for her. He is being robbed of his independence: his self-image is under attack.

This idea is reinforced when Nathan is unable to see himself in the **Mirror**. He has symbolically "lost sight" of himself. He may wish to reappraise his feelings for the girl. Is he really fond of her for who she is, or is he driven purely by lust? His feelings for her have already affected his friendship with another boy. The dream does not provide the solution but clarifies the situation. Nathan needs to learn that the most valuable relationships are based on equality, respect and understanding — not on desire, confusion and jealousy.

An adolescent's dreams often reflect concerns about the opposite sex, typically regarded as both attractive and intimidating. Hair is a common symbol of masculine self-image — hence a haircut can be deeply threatening. Such anxiety dreams can help young minds to grow in maturity through self-knowledge.

Landscape & Place

Dream symbols of place can be highly evocative. In dreams we often wander through the landscape of our memories, redolent of long-forgotten (or half-remembered) hopes, fears and longings. The past haunts us, because it has helped to create us, and it is places to which our dream selves tend to gravitate.

However, as well as the settings of **some of our deepest memories, dreams are also adept** at conjuring totally new topographies. Mansions, remote country cottages, streets bright with strange stores, towering cliffs with hidden caves – these ingredients can occur unexpectedly, often with a symbolism that is every bit as important as the symbolism of the past.

As with all attempts at interpretation, consider the most obvious associations first when intrepreting place – for example, a library might suggest a thirst for knowledge or a wish for seclusion. Look for secondary meanings too by exploring what we **might call the "penumbra" surrounding a symbol** – the ambience of less expected nuances. As no one could possibly read all the books in a library, perhaps this setting might reflect a fear that you are not making the most of all the experiences that are potentially available to you.

The character and detail of a place matter enormously, of course. Let's say that you have dreamed about a valley. Was it dry (sterility?), was there a trickle of a stream (refreshment?) or was it lush and green (fertility?). Are you surrounded by jagged crags (aggression? perhaps the fear of being swallowed if they look like teeth?) or rounded hills (again, fertility? or perhaps the easy life, without risks?).

A rural landscape can evoke conflicting feelings: we can be drawn to its beauty, its wildness, its isolation, while at the same time being unsettled by the absence of amenities, comfort, security or entertainment.

Cities, of course, can also be contradictory in the responses they elicit. Frequent associations include artifice, commerce, communications, humanity at large, and competitiveness. Again, you may have different emotional responses depending on any issues preying on your mind. If you can identify the quarter of the city you are in (commercial, bohemian, tourist trail), that can open up some interesting perspectives.

Claustrophobia and agorophobia are, in waking life, **common responses respectively to places that are too crowded and confined,** or too empty and open. In our emotional lives we may feel these discomforts by metaphorical extension: we can feel trapped or exposed in a relationship, or by a lack of one. The dreaming mind seizes upon this metaphorical language, and uses it expressively. It is always worth asking yourself whether a place you have dreamed about seems overcrowded or eerily empty: that could be the main point.

For example, let us say you have dreamed of being in a school playground. If you are alone there, that is a remarkable anomaly, as playgrounds tend to be used by groups of children or by families. The fact of being alone in a place that is normally well populated could be no less significant in the dream than the fact that your adult self seems to have regressed to childhood.

As always, when interpreting a place in a dream, you need to bear in mind the different experiences that are common to such places in general, then, even more importantly, your *own particular experiences* in them, or your own preconceptions about them.

Obviously, an agnostic feels differently about churches than a believer. But even to those of us with spiritual aspirations, churches may speak of transcendence or of our feelings of unworthiness, depending on our state of mind. Train stations and airports may hold the promise of travel and new experiences, or be places in which we are stalled, or **disorientated by a disturbing jumble** of destinations, departures and arrivals. Some people associate airports with fear of flying, or with incidents of lost luggage, forgotten passports or endless delays. In all public transport we surrender control to a system in which we are required to have faith, and this provides a fruitful line of enquiry in dream interpretation.

Dream Workshop No. 10

The Dreamer

Paul is a 21-year-old student. He has recently broken up with his girlfriend, and she is now with someone else, but Paul misses her desperately, is regretting his decision and can't stop himself from longing for more time with her.

THE DREAM

Paul is swimming in a vast, choppy, red sea, which stretches endlessly into the distance. The water is hot, and he can taste the salt on his skin as he dives effortlessly through the waves. Excited, he dives deep underwater, passing beautiful mermaids feeding each other grapes and succulent pomegranates, which makes him feel angry. He swims past other bizarre sea creatures, as well as huge red plants with many-toothed blooms and prickly stems. When he stretches his hand out to touch the flowers, they snap shut like Venus flytraps. Reaching the bottom, he finds himself in a lovely underwater garden. Heather, his ex-girlfriend, is naked in front of him, hanging out her clothes on a line — bright skirts, dresses and underwear. Unable to resist the powerful urge that seizes him, he grabs the clothes from the line between his teeth and floats to the surface to get more air.

INTERPRETATION

The interconnected symbolism in this dream might invite Paul to look more closely at some of his underlying attitudes toward women. **Mermaids** — fantasy creatures — typically symbolize a view of women that combines beauty, mystery, a siren-like allure and danger. This may suggest that Paul fantasizes about women's unattainable beauty but also feels that women are threatening and destructive emotionally.

The **Grapes** and **Pomegranates** that the mermaids are feeding to each other may represent forbidden fruits, the secret pleasures women share, from which men are excluded. The dreamer's reaction is interesting: his anger suggests fierce jealousy. Perhaps Paul needs to learn that such jealousy is pointless — each sex is inevitably excluded from sharing aspects of the other.

The **Sea Creatures** and **Strange Plants** are notable because they seem "bizarre" to Paul. They may indicate his view of women's conduct, which often seems irrational to men. The plants' **Many-toothed Blooms** and **Prickly Stems** also suggest women's capacity not only to be offended but to wound in return. **Venus Flytraps** are known for attracting and ensnaring with their beauty. However, the dreamer then descends to a **Lovely Garden**, perhaps a sign that, deep down, he is aware of another side of women — gentleness and peace.

Clothes usually symbolize the public persona and the masks we present to the world. Paul should ask himself why he was focused on Heather's clothes — the outer trappings of femininity — rather than on her unclothed (real) self. Paul **Seizes the Clothes with his Teeth**. Is this an act of aggression — a wish to hurt the person who has hurt him? Perhaps it is not Heather who has upset him, but what she represents to him. His need for **Air** at the end of the dream may reveal a certain conflict between commitment to women and a desire for freedom.

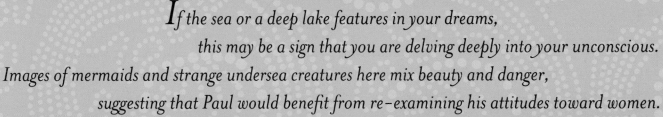

If the sea or a deep lake features in your dreams,
this may be a sign that you are delving deeply into your unconscious.
Images of mermaids and strange undersea creatures here mix beauty and danger,
suggesting that Paul would benefit from re-examining his attitudes toward women.

Buildings & Conveyances

Buildings loom large in our lives — for many of us, they are seldom out of our sight. They can represent shelter, order, civilization, status. The home is part of our sense of identity, as it contains our possessions and provides the context of much of our lives. All around us are buildings that map out our inner and outer lives: streets, shopping malls, places of worship, offices, schools, gyms, museums, cinemas, all of which have obvious associations derived from their individual purposes. With such instantly recognizable symbolism, it is easy to see why buildings feature so often in our dreams.

Buildings admit or block light in various ways, and this can be a clue to their dream significance. When you come across a dark or ill-lit environment, a basic question to ask is: what would light mean, if it were to appear in the scene? If it means knowledge, insight, understanding, as so often in everyday metaphor, then darkness conversely suggests ignorance or incomprehension. If light means love, darkness evokes loneliness, actual or imagined.

In an unfamiliar public building in waking life, we all have to use observation and reasoning to navigate a path — whether to a hotel room or to an office we are visiting for the first time. Hence strange buildings in dreams often involve an element of searching. It is reasonable to ask if such a dream refers to some kind of quest and, if so, what it might be that we are looking for.

As we move around a building, we might wonder what lies behind closed doors, take a wrong turn, find ourselves trapped, or have an unwelcome encounter on the stairs — all experiences that can crop up in dreams with hidden metaphorical significance.

The unexpected may carry a whole range of possible symbolism, according to whether the surprise is pleasant or disturbing. Often it appears to question our preconceptions. Say we dream of entering a forbidding-looking building, only to find that it opens out onto a lovely garden, with a view of hills and woods. Perhaps this scenario is reminding us that a prospect we initially find formidable may turn out to be rewarding. Similarly, if we dream of an inviting building (a friend's house, or a place of entertainment) and find something alarming inside (anything from missing floorboards to blood dripping from the ceiling), it might be wise to question some of our more optimistic assumptions.

Community or isolation?

Progress or entrapment?

A building in a dream can be ruined, neglected or under construction — always a cue for interpretation. Ask yourself whether the reference might be to your relationship with yourself (your health, any personal projects, morality, spirituality) or with other people (your commitment, compassion, communication).

Along with buildings, "conveyances" are one of the most common motifs in dreams. The old-fashioned term is a useful one to denote obvious vehicles such as cars, trains, buses and the like, as well as elevators, escalators, roller blades — anything that takes us from one place to another. The category also includes objects we use to carry things, such as shopping trolleys, suitcases, wheelbarrows, but also telephones and computers, which convey voices and information.

One of the most important qualities behind conveyances in dreams, is the idea of change. If we are on the move, the reference might be to a change in our lives (our occupation, social circle, activities, outlook or beliefs), whether actual or desired — or feared. The speed and suitability of this change may be symbolized by the speed and suitability of the conveyance.

In addition, using a cart, wheelbarrow or suitcase to move something can, according to context, suggest new experiences or ridding ourselves of something, such as responsibility, work or mistaken ideas.

Conveyances that take us up or down, such as elevators or escalators, are thought by some to represent faint memories of out-of-body experiences (see pp.161-162), but more usually they are thought to symbolize progress without effort — one is carried up or down by the force of events.

Telephones and computers may denote some distant action that affects you, or a desire to exert influence without being seen to be involved. Or they may suggest a sense of power: the ability to perform seemingly magical acts from a distance.

Dream Workshop No. 11

The Dreamer

Alexandra is a 45-year-old advertising consultant, who has been given her first movie ad to produce. She's excited about the project, but knows she must be watchful of Samuel, her 27-year-old assistant, who can sometimes have a tendency to undermine her authority.

THE DREAM

Alexandra is in the driver's seat of a train. She has a steering wheel to control it, even though it is running on tracks. The tracks do complicated loops in the air, and all around is jungle. She is wearing a top hat and has to hold it tightly onto her head every time the train loops a loop. In the train are giraffes, monkeys and lions. Alexandra has the important mission of taking them to job interviews at the local circus. Suddenly, the tracks ahead of her start changing into snakes. One of the snakes hisses a warning that a dangerous artist has escaped from an asylum. Alexandra swings the wheel to one side to avoid the snakes and comes off the track. She knows that without the track to direct its journey, the train will end up back where it started.

INTERPRETATION

The muddled imagery in this dream may reflect the complications of Alexandra's professional life, but the questions it raises could prove very useful. The **Steering Wheel** clearly relates to her sense of control. To some extent she is able to influence the way she is going. Yet the steering wheel is incongruous in a **Train Running on Tracks**: she also has to go where the rails take her.

Is she really in control of what is happening at work, or is she propelled by circumstances? The rails are also unreliable, making **Loops in the Air** as if they wish to take off from the ground. The steering wheel suggests a car, but the tracks suggest a train and the loops in the air a plane. How does she want to travel and where exactly does she hope to be heading? The ending of the dream underlines the importance of these questions. Does she fear ending up back where she started?

The **Top Hat** may be a symbol of authority, yet Alexandra has to hold on to it every time the train goes into a loop. She may be insecure about her position and anxious about a loss of control.

Animals often represent instincts, but in this context Alexandra might consider if these specific animals mean anything else to her. **Giraffes** sometimes symbolize far-sightedness, **Monkeys** mischief and greed, and **Lions** courage and royalty. The animals are going for interviews, which suggests competition. A choice will have to be made between the qualities they each represent.

The **Snake** symbolizes contradictory qualities in all the great cultural traditions, but in the West it usually represents deceit and danger. The snake is giving Alexandra advice, but can it be trusted? The warning is about a dangerous **Artist** who has **Escaped from an Asylum**. There is a suggestion here that creativity can be dangerous and even lead to madness. What can Alexandra do to make her professional life more goal-directed and secure? Whom can she trust? How can she ensure that her work is well-grounded?

*S*ome dreams seem specifically designed to cause confusion.
To make sense out of the mix, start by focusing on individual elements.
The train, top hat, animals and escaped artist here seem to be disconnected symbols,
but through association the thread of personal meaning may become clear.

Actions

All sorts of actions feature in our dreams, from playing games and chopping wood to walking and brushing our hair. We might also dream of some actions, such as flying, that we cannot do ordinarily in waking life.

Most actions involve movement, which can symbolize many things. If rapid or dramatic, it can indicate transformation from one situation or condition to another. If in slow motion, as in some nightmares, it may reflect helplessness. If exhilarating, it may show that change might be liberating – particularly when the dreamer flies or floats unaided. Such dreams can remind us that many things are possible if we believe in ourselves. Sometimes, in flight, the dreamer may ask others to witness the feat, perhaps hinting that we are trying to convince our doubting side that we can succeed. While he was lying gravely ill, Jung had a dream of flying to a place of beauty – such images, on Level Three, may foreshadow the soul leaving the body to travel to its spiritual home.

One of our most expressive actions is dancing, which in dreams often symbolizes freedom from care and points to the unfounded nature of many everyday worries.

Dreams of climbing can suggest aspirations to new areas of life, whereas falling can indicate insecurities about our ambition.

Not surprisingly, for most dream actions, context is key. Running is a good example. This can be enjoyable in dreams and may represent progress, especially if we are racing ahead of others. But we may find ourselves running *away* from or *toward* something. Establish *why* you are running, then ask yourself what associations that brings. Running *after* something can suggest anxiety or frustration, in which case the object chased usually gives a clue to the nature of the problem: a ball may suggest a wish to recapture lost childhood. However, if you are chasing your car, you may feel out of control. Reflect on whether you succeed in catching the object and whether you wanted to catch it in the first place.

Riding a bicycle in dreams is often said to be a sexual symbol, but it can have other interpretations. Cycling slowly up a steep hill might reflect some sort of struggle in your life, whereas if you are freewheeling down a slope, you may be relishing the thought of breaking away from current circumstances and enjoying a new opportunity.

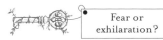

Fear or exhilaration?

Travelling offers a number of aspects for consideration: the vehicle, the route, the view, the speed, the company, and any activity you engage in apart from simply moving. Your feelings about the journey are all-important. Think about what you are leaving behind as well as your destination. In dreams of riding a horse or other animal, the animal's characteristics can give clues to the meaning. In dreams of swimming or climbing, the elemental setting tends to be full of significance.

Eating or drinking can be simple wish-fulfilment – many dieters dream of "forbidden" foods. Consumption may symbolize a need for social, emotional or intellectual stimulation. Food and drink can represent what we are taking from the world, such as financial rewards, or even the treatment we receive from loved ones. Being forced to eat **may symbolize being "force-fed" by** well-meaning but **misguided family or friends.**

Music is ubiquitous today, so it is strange that dreams of singing are rarely reported.

Singing, like dancing, is linked to emotional release, so reluctance to sing may suggest a fear of expressing emotions. Any creative art may indicate a desire to try to improve the world.

When shopping in a dream, you might see **enticing objects that are always out of reach,** representing frustrated **ambition or longing.** Desirable items for sale can represent temptation. Giving or receiving items can reflect our relationships with others: giving a gift indicates positive feelings toward a person, yet lavishing presents on them may connote inappropriate social conduct. Receiving very few gifts on a birthday may reflect insecurity with friends.

Competitive sport, or fighting, may have as much to do with the opponent as with the action itself. As for partying, notice how others react to us and how we feel about ourselves. Needing to use the toilet in public and finding it occupied, or, worse, relieving ourselves in the wrong place, can point to a deep fear of doing the wrong thing or unburdening ourselves emotionally.

Dream Workshop No. 12

The Dreamer

Eddie, 23, has just completed a gap year after finishing university. He has been travelling the world, experiencing new cultures, and is apprehensive about having to find a job and settle down to "normality".

THE DREAM

Eddie is making his way through the jungle, looking for a medicine man — someone who knows the secret of flight. He senses that it will soon start to get dark. Everything around him feels strange, and he's scared to be so far from camp. He hears the loud roar of animals all around and worries that something might attack him. Then suddenly he's by a fire with the medicine man and a group of young tribesmen, all wearing animal skins and animal headdresses. They seem to be preparing for an initiation ceremony. There is a leopard with them, which rears up on its hind legs. Eddie knows he's not allowed to join in, so he feels frustrated and disappointed. But the medicine man gives him a large, brightly coloured feather and sets a sheet of blank paper on the ground, whereupon Eddie sits down and starts drawing the scene instead, using the feather as a pen, and this makes him feel much better.

INTERPRETATION

The dream gives a strong sense of the tropical **Jungle**. Even if Eddie did not visit the tropics, the dream's vibrancy and strangeness may simply come from his mind assimilating the exotic experiences of his gap year into his frame of reference. However, the jungle also suggests confusion, lack of direction and sometimes a sense of danger, which ties in with the dreamer's current apprehension about the future. This possibility is rendered more likely by his fear of **Darkness**, which suggests the unknown.

The **Tribesmen** may represent the group of friends Eddie hopes to meet in his future job. The sense that he cannot join in the initiation may imply that he worries about being excluded. Their costumes are significant. Freud suggested that **Animals** often symbolize the dreamer's instinctive self. The tribesmen are all wearing animal skins. Perhaps they feel comfortable with their instincts, whereas Eddie worries that his might overwhelm him — he fears that animals might attack.

There are two possible archetypal figures here, which are closely associated: the **Leopard** is a powerful symbol of ferocity and magical powers; and the **Medicine Man** may have some of the symbolism of the Wise Old Man. The fact that the leopard is on its hind legs strengthens the impression that it may represent a power animal, a creature that leads the shaman to the other world.

Eddie needs to ask himself why he wanted to meet the medicine man. Is he searching for guidance about something? If so, it is probably significant that the medicine man does not tell Eddie anything, but gives him a **Feather**. In South American tradition, the feather symbolizes truth and ascending to higher realms. Eddie uses the medicine man's gift to discover that he has been enriched by his experiences, and that his destiny may lie in some sort of creative work.

*M*any dreams raise more questions than answers. It is impossible to ascribe a precise meaning to the feather, or to explain why it can be used as a pen even without ink. But achieving the impossible is usually a positive sign in a dream, suggesting that there are ways to resolve our issues. Exploring possible meanings of the dream's symbolism is a constructive first step.

Nature

In our largely artificial environment it is easy to forget that we come from the natural world and depend upon it for our survival. Dreams, on the other hand, do not forget this. Our unconscious is well aware of our roots, and of our deep longing to reconnect with nature.

When interpreting dream memories, do not fall into the trap of concentrating solely on the obviously human content. If the dream has a natural setting, the natural details could have a noteworthy symbolic value.

Quite apart from specific associations, nature often has general significance in dreams, as the life-force, the energizing vitality that drives the cycle of birth, death and renewal. If you are receptive to such influences from the dream world, the waking world can also take on a new vibrancy: you may even find that you start each new day with refreshed enthusiasm.

The ancients recognized four so-called elements – fire, earth, air and water – and these are primal ingredients of the collective unconscious. Although no longer accepted by science, they have a rich symbolism that will never become obsolete.

Fire denotes the complementary opposites of destruction and creation: it can devastate but is also crucial for survival, giving warmth as well as clearing land as a preparation for fresh growth. Traditionally, it signifies passion. Earth is the grounding element that keeps us real – the bedrock of our existence. Rock itself can represent eternity, and by extension permanence, emotional stability, strength. Like fire, it has its ambiguities: it can be unyielding, unresponsive to change. Air is the spirit that breathes life into our lungs, while the wind brings change and renewal. Of course, being generally invisible, air will not feature so obviously in a dream as the other three elements, but look out for subtle manifestations: moving clouds or rustling leaves that indicate a breeze, or a lover's breath felt on the skin. Water traditionally embodies purity and cleansing, and offers a lesson in dealing with obstacles: that is, find a way around them rather than confronting them. Other associations of water are the unconscious itself (with its oceanic depths), purity, peace and sustenance.

The elements give in summary form an excellent overview of how we experience the tangible world, including our own bodies.

Trees → Life? Growth? Stability? Refuge? Strength?

Fish

Good luck?
Fertility?
Fluidity?
Creativity?
Rebirth?

Clouds

Transience?
Lightness?
Obscurity?
Threat?
Renewal?

If you hold the idea of the elements in your mind as you drift into sleep, this can encourage your unconscious to bring out these basic natural connections in your dreams.

Freud and his followers saw nature as a source of sexual symbols — waves and water as the sexual act; valleys and caves as the female genitals, mountains and high places as the male genitals. But in fact, mountains are aspirational. They have always represented our ascent to a higher world, while valleys suggest fertility, comfort and safety. Mountains often symbolize masculinity, valleys femininity, without necessarily any sexual implication.

Trees can stand for majesty and strength, the family (branching generations), the promise of shelter and warmth. Individual species add their own particular meanings: the willow denotes flexibility, and perhaps also sadness (because of the weeping willow); the yew, being common in churchyards and having dark foliage, has connotations of mortality. Wordplay may operate: if a pine tree appears in a dream, the reference could be to the word "pine", meaning lament, as much as to the tree itself.

Flowers imply fragility and transient beauty — though some, of course, are perennial, with a prospect of renewal. They also suggest hope and optimism, but we have to be aware too of the funereal associations of some flowers, such as lilies.

When the symbolism of nature flows through our dreams, we must be alert to a whole range of interpretative possibilities, instead of opting for simplistic one-for-one choices based on traditional symbolism — or even the more familiar ambiguities that some aspects of nature universally bring with them. The personal can override or compromise the universal, or give it a particular tinge of its own. Water, for one dreamer, may evoke a bad childhood experience of a near-drowning in a storm at sea while sailing. Another dreamer might have spent many happy years fly-fishing in a placid lake. An important point here is that even still water — reflecting an idyllic view of sky or forest — can act as a trigger of alarm for that first dreamer, whose unconscious perhaps remembers a deceptively calm sea before the storm blew up. The second dreamer, the fly-fisher, may have memories of a sad event at the lakeside — a parting from a lover, say

— that overlays with pain her otherwise happy memories. Personal experience can add an extra layer of complexity to an already quite complex symbolic vocabulary.

Any aspect of the landscape can have personal associations, either by the accident of proximity (the fly-fisher) or by an incident in which nature played a leading role (the sailor). The elements potentially lend themselves to both these categories. Accidents or near-accidents with fire and water are both very common. Fire does not often rage freely in nature, so a fruitful line of enquiry by the intrepreter is often a campfire (especially in childhood) and the family hearth. If neither seems applicable, the commonplace association with anger (a negative side of passion) is perhaps most likely. You may be afraid of losing control over your own anger, or you may once have been frightened of the anger of others — a parent or teacher possibly. Bad experiences with air tend to have more to do with fear of flying than with cyclones or gales. Earth may suggest a universal deep-seated anxiety about being buried

alive, connecting with unease about our own mortality; at a personal level it may recall worries about being smothered as a child. All this shades into nightmare if the emotions of the sleeping mind are especially intense.

However, the personal symbolism associated with nature, like the universal symbolism, is usually more positive. Even if we are unable to identify any links with particular life experiences, we may feel a special connection with nature as a whole or with specific aspects of it: flowers may simply denote both celebration and sympathy; warmth from a fire suggests welcome and hospitality; lakes or rivers evoke ideas of relaxation and leisure.

The sun, moon and stars definitely lie in the realm of the universal. The sun, seen as kingly in antiquity, is masculine, extroverted, powerful, predictable; the queenly moon is mysterious, erratic, magical, intuitive. We all have both sun and moon in our pyschological make-up to some degree. Sunlight is the medium of our outer life, while our inner self is arguably more lunar. Stars link with destiny, aspirations, remoteness and, inevitably today, celebrity.

Display?
Aggression?
Exoticism?
Repetitiveness?
Ego?

Parrot

Bookishness?
Wisdom?
Solitude?
Mystery?
Predation?

Owl

Nobility?
Co-operation?
Power?
Speed?
Intelligence?

Horse

Independence?
Sensuality?
Comfort?
Stealth?
Agility?

Cat

Deer

Shyness?
Vulnerability?
Wildness?
Freedom?
Grace?

Animals

Animals carry centuries of traditional symbolism, as well as emotional and personal associations that may affect the meaning when they occur in dreams. For example, the lion is an age-old emblem of courage, but if you dream about one there may be other factors at work. Lions could perhaps provoke fear, or admiration for their majesty, or you may think of them as embodiments of strong independence. Or it may be that you have recently walked over a rug that reminded you, subliminally, of a lion's pelt. If so, the question still arises, why did that detail persist in your unconscious mind? Might your deep-rooted memory of this reflect something of significance?

Similar ambiguities surround, for example, the owl: denoting wisdom, it is also a ruthless predator, active in a silent, dark world. Or does it suggest bookishness? If so, this could be an aspiration toward learning or fear of withdrawal from real life. The snake, similarly, slithers through a tangle of meanings, including guile, stealth, grace, betrayal, invisibility, phallic energy and — because it sloughs off its skin — renewal.

Foxes stand for cunning, rats and pigs tend to suggest dirt or squalor (unfairly in the case of the latter). Cats symbolize stealth and independence, but they are also widely kept as pets, and therefore personal references may be intended. Kittens tend to be playful or naughty. Dogs may evoke warm personal feelings, with a strong hint of loyalty, though they can also be sources of fear. Remember that the death of a pet is often a child's first experience of grief, and the trauma may be buried deep in the unconscious.

Animals are the stock-in-trade of children's stories, and their importance in this respect has rippled through the dream world. Memories of bedtime storytelling sessions can be the key to animal dreams that otherwise might seem impenetrable.

Freud regarded animals as symbols of our instincts — our unlearned, unconditioned self. If you find yourself thinking along these lines, try to identify from the context whether the dream is suggesting that your instincts should be more freely expressed or more controlled.

Sacred before Christianity, fish represent fertility, renewal, even rebirth. They can occur in Level Three dreams (as can mythical beasts like the unicorn or dragon), and may be a token of profound insights.

Objects

The dreaming mind seems happy to present a relatively realistic backdrop to most of our dreams — one that helps to set the tone of the dream and supplement the symbolism of any objects that appear. Thus a car usually represents travel, but when set in a harsh, industrial landscape, it may also allude to a need to escape; or in a pleasant rural scene, the urge to explore. Objects can be interpreted effectively only if you take their context fully into account.

After looking at the object in relation to the dream as a whole, it may help to place it in an appropriate category: domestic; work and professional; creativity and information; clothing; leisure and hobbies; weapons. Note anything unusual about the dream object, as well as your emotional response to it.

Domestic items are among the most common objects to appear in dreams. We handle them daily, without giving them much thought, and repetition of this kind is a sure way to make an impact on the unconscious. They are things we often hand to others in the home, and therefore may have some connection in a dream with relationships. Of all dream objects, they are the most likely to have incongruous features, in a way that can

lend itself readily to interpretation. A teapot with no spout, for example, may symbolize that you expect to be welcomed (the teapot), but end up disappointed (no spout). Soup simmering in a conjuror's top hat might suggest nourishment or support (the soup) that turns out to be trickery (the top hat). A living room full of tennis rackets may allude to leisure time that has been restricted by domestic commitments. A computer with a mirror instead of a screen may suggest a reluctance to look beyond self-interest.

When at Level One we dream of objects realistically, they may be there as a focus of anxious or excited feelings about some forthcoming event. Then again, if they are significant objects in the home, we may simply be having guilty feelings about them — for example, a chair you dream about might be one you have been meaning for some time to get re-upholstered; a grandfather clock might be one that annoys your husband with its off-key chimes.

The work environment potentially offers many richly symbolic objects to the dreaming mind — everything from calculators to filing cabinets. In the workplace an item such as a chair or desk can acquire an inflated

Decorative
or useful?

importance as an emblem of status, and this is something to look out for in dreams if you have worries about your career or about the hierarchy at your place of work. Locked desk drawers, to which the keys have been lost, may suggest anxieties about your access to information, while a spectacularly untidy desk may point to a nagging feeling that your career path is not being managed well.

Items linked with creativity (paintbrushes, musical instruments and the like) may take us by surprise in dreams if we do not think of ourselves as creative people. The truth is, however, that we are *all* creative. Often we neglect the artistic side of ourselves, through lack of encouragement in childhood and in later life. But creative activities can surface in dreams, perhaps indicating frustrated creative impulses.

Objects that are *used* — that is, tools or instruments of some kind — often carry overtones of performance, which can bring many feelings into play, from shame that you are unable to fly a kite to determination to get a cork out of a bottle with a corkscrew. One of the most satisfying dreams of this kind is finding yourself able

to play an instrument you have never learned — a positive message from your unconscious that it is time to acknowledge your hidden creative aspirations and seek an outlet for them. Possession of exciting magical objects, such as shoes that enable you to fly across the countryside, can also indicate strong creative urges.

All objects may stand at times for things other than themselves, and this is particularly true of dreams involving weapons. Freudian dream interpretation tends to suggest that weapons are symbolic of male sexuality — particularly types that penetrate, such as knives, or ejaculate, such as handguns. However, there are other possibilities. At face value weapons might suggest frustration and aggression, perhaps linked to problems and conflicts at work, or in relationships; but if we look deeper, they may be linked to a strong desire for change, breaking out of conventional ways of thinking to head off in a new direction. Weapons can also represent power, the urge to fight back against injustice, or merely a wish to attract attention.

Dreams featuring objects linked with death are not

Top hat

Formality?
Absurdity?
Pomposity?
Disguise?
Authority?

Watch

Punctuality?
Value?
Regularity?
Heartbeat?
Anxiety?

Liberation or
Destruction?

Celebration?
Sadness?
Tenderness?
Transience?
Beauty?

Shoes

Sexuality?
Dominance?
Limitation?
Protection?
Stability?

Petals

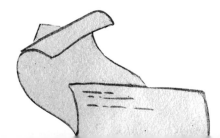

unusual. Coffins, gravestones, even corpses and dead hands and faces, are among the things reported. They can be terrifying while dreaming, and on awakening may cause fear of actual death, but associations often reveal that the true meaning has to do with change and renewal. Death is a precursor to rebirth: in Hindu teachings Shiva, the god of destruction, is also the god of change. Dead cut flowers, however, can represent aridity, something precious that has faded through neglect. The same can be true of any object that crumbles into dust when touched.

A category of object with completely different associations is toys, which some people dream about often. Most obviously, they stand for childhood and possibly our wish to return to the comfort and security of that time (which is not to say that *every* childhood has these values). But toys can be deceptive. Dolls may suggest motherhood, or they may imply that someone is rather static and wooden, or undeveloped. Toy soldiers may suggest regimentation, while toy cars, or any toys that represent expensive objects in real life, may hint at pretensions to be more wealthy or successful than is the case.

Common objects may symbolize different things to different people. To a practical-minded person, machinery may stand for progress, while to a romantic it might mean inhumanity. Other objects, such as jewels, have traditional associations, which the unconscious may borrow. Diamonds represent eternity and clarity; sapphires, truth and peacefulness; emeralds, the natural world and hope; rubies, royalty, power and passion. A collection of jewels denotes hidden treasure or wisdom. Gold often symbolizes majesty, light and masculinity, whereas silver conjures mystery, darkness and femininity.

Receiving a letter in a dream may convey a message through the identity of the sender, or the unexpectedness of a parcel may point to new challenges ahead. Delivering letters may indicate a sense of power over others.

If a dream object proves difficult to interpret, think about what it is for. Is it being used for that purpose? Is it effective? Does it attract or repel? To whom does it belong? Might it have sexual significance (see p.72)? If no answers emerge, put the question aside: the unconscious may reveal the meaning when you least expect it.

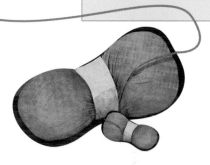

Dream Workshop No. 13

The Dreamer

Jason is a 40-year-old travel agent and a bachelor. He had an argument with his sister a few months ago, after she'd hinted that he was antisocial and unhelpful as an uncle. He wonders if he may have overreacted, but he has not yet mustered the effort to apologize.

THE DREAM

Jason is standing in his old school classroom, wearing an outdated uniform, which is too small and feels uncomfortable. Beside him is a blackboard with a drawing of the world on it. Hanging from the ceiling is his pride and joy — a vintage Harley-Davidson motorcycle. He is aware that a lesson is about to start, so he withdraws to the back of the class to sit down, waiting with trepidation for the teacher to arrive. The door opens and a female traffic cop walks in. "Today's lesson," she says, "is all about how to wrap presents with nice paper and ribbons. First, show me what you can do."

Jason takes a frog from his pocket and tries to wrap it in his handkerchief, but the frog keeps jumping out of the wrapping. Then the traffic cop starts to write in her notebook, and he assumes she's reporting him for a poor performance. She asks him his name, and he answers "General Motors" to throw her off the scent. She salutes him, blows on a whistle and tells him that the state has no alternative but to take possession of his motorcycle. A crowd of children run into the room and start taking the bike down from the ceiling. Before they finish, the school bell rings and he awakens, only to realize that it is the sound of his alarm clock.

THE INTERPRETATION

The context of Jason's dream, the **Classroom**, suggests that his sister's recent criticisms may have "put him in his place" and touched on issues that extend back to his childhood. However, the classroom is an incongruous place for an adult. His **Ill-Fitting Uniform** may indicate that he does not fully accept the situation.

Jason's anxious anticipation of the arrival of the **Teacher** suggests a childish fear of authority, particularly that which comes from outward trappings rather than inner qualities. This idea is extended when the teacher turns out to be a traffic cop. Jason should consider his relationship with his sister. Is he perhaps in awe of her?

The task of **Wrapping Presents** is often delegated to women, so Jason might perceive it as a threat to his masculinity. However, his response is ineffectual. The object he takes from his pocket is a **Frog**, a creature symbolizing elusiveness and Jason's own lack of authority. In an effort not to appear feminine, he has no "nice" wrapping paper and ribbons. He tries to use his **Handkerchief**, but this is an inappropriate item here.

Jason attempts to reclaim power by associating himself with a large motor manufacturer. Symbols of masculinity reassure him. His **Motorcycle** suggests the security that a child seeks in his toys, its high position showing his attempt to elevate its importance. A vintage model, it epitomizes strength and virility. However, the traffic cop eventually confiscates it, and children take it down, demonstrating its fallibility as a symbol of manhood.

*W*hat happens to an object in a dream can be just as important as what happens to a person.
Here, children and a female figure take control of the masculine motorcycle,
revealing the dreamer's deep awareness that true happiness does not come from possessions,
or totems of power, and that it may be time for him to focus on family and relationships.

Numbers

Numbers are among the most intriguing facts of existence. Physical reality itself is best understood in terms of mathematical models, and the universe seems to have obeyed mathematical principles from the first instant of creation. Numerology grew up around the belief that divination was possible through numbers, and even today much remains to be discovered about the way numbers behave and relate to each other.

In dreams numbers may play an archetypal role, and it is interesting to note those that occur or recur. A house or bus may have a number (personal associations may be at work here) and sometimes people appear in groups of an identifiable number. A dream character may repeat a word or action a set number of times.

One approach to interpreting dream numbers is to identify, initially, whether they are odd or even. Many cultures see odd numbers as active and masculine, and even numbers as passive and feminine — given that we all have masculine and feminine sides, there is no gender bias in this assertion.

"Active" refers to the fact that odd numbers tend to be unstable and liable to movement, while even numbers are more stable and static — a tripod is less stable than a quadrapod. In dreams odd numbers may suggest a need for action, while even numbers may stress the need for balance and harmony.

Use either free or direct association (see pp.49–50) to interpret individual numbers, or consider whether established meanings strike any chords. Traditionally, one represents the origin, the cause of all things; two stands for the fertile union of opposites; three for the divine trinity and the triad of mind, body and soul; four for the earth and perfect balance; five for humankind (humans have four limbs and a head); six (the sum of the first three divine numbers) for realization and perfection; seven for the union of heaven and earth; eight for regeneration and rebirth; nine (three times three) for completion and attainment; and ten for the sum of all possibilities. Zero symbolizes not only emptiness, but eternity, without beginning or end.

4

Guide to Dream Logic

At first sight, dreams make little sense — a hammer might turn into a snake, you might be lost in a maze of shadows, or it might be raining custard. However, no matter how bizarre the dream, we accept it at the time. Dreams reshape the logic by which we live, and in doing so remind us that we should not take our waking realities too much for granted.

Introduction to Dream Logic

There are two kinds of logic: *deductive* and *inductive*. Deductive logic consists of a premise followed by a factual statement, then a conclusion. A familiar example is: "All men are mortal. Socrates is a man. Therefore Socrates is mortal." Inductive logic, as used in science (and by the fictional detective Sherlock Holmes), starts with evidence, then draws conclusions: "There is confetti outside the church. Confetti is thrown at weddings. Therefore there has been a wedding."

We all use both kinds of logic to make sense of our world and to reach conclusions that help us to function in life.

The dream world, for the most part, obeys the rules neither of deductive nor of inductive logic. This is puzzling: it is difficult to see why the unconscious should go its own way. But we can begin to understand how dream logic works by seeing if our dreams create their own sets of rules.

The first thing you may notice is that dreams care little about veracity of detail. For example, you may dream of your bedroom, yet the dream places the windows in the wrong position, or two windows appear instead of one. Or you may dream of someone you know, yet their appearance is different —

interestingly, this does not prevent you from recognizing them. Or you may find that a skill at which you are proficient in waking life, such as playing the guitar, is beyond you. These errors of detail are usually noticed only when you recall the dream the next morning. While dreaming, you just accept them.

You may also notice that dreams do not care about consistency in any way. Not only may the details of a scene change within a dream, or from one dream to another, but also the objects or figures in your dreams may transform themselves, even while you look at them. A furry hat may become a horse, a friend may change into a stranger, a book may sprout flowers. The dreaming mind accepts these transformations without surprise. (Learning to notice such changes helps a dream to become "lucid", as we see later, in Chapter 6.)

Dreams flout not only the law of identity (one thing in a dream may turn into another) but also the laws of space and time. A friend of mine had a dream in which he was travelling alone by train in Eastern Europe, heading for a place named Plin (which he afterwards discovered does not exist). He was due to meet his brother there, who was travelling

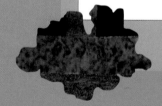

separately from Prague. The train stopped in the middle of the night in an empty landscape. Knowing there was no hope of another train, he got out with his suitcase and started walking. Suddenly, he came across a signpost saying, "Fisher's Green 2 miles." He was back on familiar ground, about 10 miles from his home in London, near a small country park. He called his brother on his cell phone to say that he would be unable to meet him in Plin after all.

This was the dream — no more, no less. The question could be asked: Is it time or space in this dream that is distorted? This can be answered only after a little thought, because the dream has no reference either to the distance covered or to the time taken: it omits the experience of walking. Perhaps the best response is to say that *both* dimensions are distorted, because neither registers realistically. On top of this, there is distortion in the rules of polite conduct: no apology is given for the failure to meet. Then again, if we look at what the dream actually entails, carrying a suitcase from Eastern Europe to the United Kingdom also rather stretches credulity. Some magic must be at work: the magic of the unconscious.

This example is typical, but many dreams occur, especially Level One dreams, in which thoughts and actions do remain relatively true to waking life. Frequently in dreams we still act in accordance with our usual sense of right and wrong. We also tend to maintain our sense of self, knowing who we are even if we appear younger or older than in reality. We also tend to experience our normal pattern of emotions. Thus, although dreams seem unconcerned about extraneous details, they have no difficulty in representing our essential nature.

With this in mind, it may be that dreams use their inconsistencies to teach us valuable lessons about ourselves, about other people, or about some other aspect of our lives. In general terms, they remind us that the world, although it may look solid enough, is in a constant state of change, and our place within it is unstable. In many ways the dreaming mind represents a far more discerning part of our consciousness than the waking mind. Undistracted by the perpetual activity of the physical world, it retires into itself and accesses many of the secrets behind the puzzle of existence. Perhaps in dreaming we draw closer to ultimate realities.

Dream Workshop No. 14

The Dreamer

Kate, a busy 44-year-old, is worried that she doesn't know enough about how her two teenage daughters are spending their time, and fears that their friends might be unsuitable.

THE DREAM

There are three striped tents in the desert, of elaborate, pavilion-like construction. Camels are grazing near them. However, other elements of the scene suggest the Wild West: there's a saloon, with horses tethered outside, and honky-tonk music drifts through the saloon doors. A bank is under construction, and there are dollar signs around its facade. A bearded man on a ladder is painting fake windows on the bank using black paint. A doctor selling snake-oil medicine from a temporary booth has a long queue of people waiting to be served. Some of the people who have already bought medicine are doing cartwheels in the dirt road; others are turning green and falling down sick.

THE INTERPRETATION

The **Tents** provide a vital clue to understanding this dream. Tents represent concealment, and if Kate's daughters are not confiding in her, she needs to know the reason. Certainly, there are aspects of their relationship that need attention. But it seems that there is more to the dream than this. There are **Three** tents, one for the dreamer as well. Kate may be the one who uses her tent as a place in which to hide, perhaps reflecting her relationships with people in general.

The **Desert** implies the present state of their family relationships, but may also indicate Kate's loneliness. **Camels** — the "ships of the desert" — are clearly the best way to cross it, but for some reason Kate is not using them, denying herself the opportunity for travel and new experiences.

The incongruous **Wild West** scenery suggests an old movie, and therefore artificiality. This idea is reinforced by the **Bank**, which usually has connotations of security, but here is more emphatically linked with money. This could alert Kate to the fact that greed and material possessions offer false promises. The bank's **Windows** are also fake: they represent concealment behind a false show of openness. Even the man's beard may be fake, a disguise behind which he hides.

The **Snake-Oil Salesman** is an untrustworthy figure, and his presence furthers the imagery of deception that the dream has established. Perhaps Kate feels that she has been let down by others in the past. She notices that some people have been taken in and are turning **Cartwheels**, a movement that looks spectacular but is not a normal or efficient way of moving forward; others turn **Green** and fall sick. (Green can symbolize the natural world, and so offers an interesting line of further enquiry.) Kate understands that deceit is not something to be "stomached". The salesman's medicine offers a false promise of inner healing. Deep down she is aware that happiness should come not from others, but from within oneself.

*T*he movies can infiltrate your unconscious and provide you with the basic elements of a dream.
When you encounter scenes remote from your own experience, it is worth asking if this might
be their source. Here, the movie-set artificiality highlights the dream's consistent message —
that Kate needs to reject deception and search for the genuine and sincere.

Dream Narrative

Dreams can sometimes feel like old friends who can't quite stick to the point. They tend to ramble. A dream that starts off at the seaside may well end up by your desk at the office, while one that starts at your desk is perfectly capable of ending up in an empty street that rings a vague bell from your childhood.

The seemingly chaotic nature of dreams is one of the reasons many people tend to dismiss them as nonsense. But if we look at the narrative of a typical waking day, we often find that this is just as illogical, with interruptions, changes of plan, sudden terminations to one activity in order to start another, and so on: to an onlooker our actions would probably appear rather haphazard.

Moreover, if we were to go further than that and start to take an honest look at our typical thought processes, we would find even more randomness. In the light of all this, it would surely not be credible that the unconscious could operate in a more orderly fashion than the conscious mind.

Dreams follow something of the disjointed pattern of waking life, but tend to be more confusing, in various ways. One of their habits is to leave out the internal links. Thus, they move from one location to another, and from one episode of the narrative to another, without covering the insignificant episodes in between. They are concerned only with whatever is relevant to their underlying content.

It is often better to think of a dream as containing several narratives, like a compilation of short stories, rather than just one. Alternatively, you may prefer to think of it as separate dreams — each of which may, in fact, be separated during the night by periods of dreamless sleep of which you are unaware. Each of these "separate" dreams or short stories may carry its own message and therefore require its own individual interpretation. On the other hand, it is often interesting as well as revealing to review all the separate episodes together and see if you can detect any kind of pattern — perhaps a progression, a contrast, or a series of parallels.

"Narrative" is a broadly useful concept to apply to dreams in an attempt to make sense of them. They often work by unfolding events, and when this happens they can be likened to stories. Yet you will usually be disppointed if you expect a clear beginning, middle and end, and a clear sense of motivation and character. If they are stories, they are ones that opt for a modernist, experimental style tinged with magical realism. But because of all the strange juxtapositions, the mysterious encounters or settings, not to mention the flashbacks in time and the special effects, some people might find it more useful to think of dreams as inner movie-making — an exploratory cinema of the mind.

A good place to start analyzing a dream narrative is to ask yourself if it has any sense of development. Take Nicole's dream of flying described in the Workshop on the following page, which progresses from an imaginary childhood reunion to an exhilarating experience of flying. There is in fact a progression that enables us to reject a different possible interpretation of the dream: the idea that Nicole should leave company behind and find selfish satisfaction in a solitary pursuit. Joy in the dream comes not only from flying, but from the enlarged perspective. Nothing would have happened without the meeting of friends in the first place. It is Nicole's friend who points out the balloons; and the exchange of gifts means that the ecstasy, when it comes, has a basis in generous conduct. The progression of actions and symbols in the dream yields a plausible analysis.

As dreams go, Nicole's is relatively coherent, with a clear narrative. Many dreams you experience will be more fragmentary. At times you may even feel that what you have dreamed is more like the original notes or sketch for a short story than the story itself. In such cases the analytical approach is still worth taking: the development could be a simple transition from one image to another. Imagine that someone dreams of a set of train tracks passing through a house and bursting into flower on the other side. Even here there is scope for interpretation, for there is a progression from a constrained forward motion to an opening out in all directions, as well as from the mechanical to the organic. The overall meaning, and the signficance of the house, will — as always — depend primarily on the dreamer.

Dream Workshop No. 15

The Dreamer

Nicole is in her early thirties. Five years ago she became divorced, which damaged her self-confidence, as her parents had divorced and she had vowed that she would never do the same. Now she has remarried, moved to a new town and feels happier than she has for a long time.

THE DREAM

Nicole is sitting in a beautiful meadow with one of her childhood friends, Monica, whom in reality she hasn't seen since junior school. They are sitting on a rug that is such a bright shade of yellow that it seems to be reflecting in their faces. They have brought each other a gift. Nicole gives Monica a bright cuddly toy, Monica gives Nicole a fancy-dress pirate hat. They play with their respective gifts, chatting and laughing. Monica smiles and points to a huge bunch of orange balloons floating up over the hill. Nicole, compelled by a strong urge, gets up to run after them. The more she runs, the more energized she feels, until she is leaping high in the sky, above fields, rivers and houses. Finally, she catches one balloon that has strayed from the pack and lets it carry her along, without a care in the world. She is still drifting contentedly in the sky when she wakes up — with a sense of disappointment to discover that in reality she is on the ground after all.

INTERPRETATION

The dream suggests a growing awareness in Nicole of the most important aspects of life. **Meadows** are interesting archetypal symbols, as they are mid-way between cultivated gardens and natural wilderness. As such, they often suggest peace, security and the desire for a simpler life. In this case Nicole is also with an **Old School Friend**. Perhaps she wishes for a return to a more innocent way of life. The friend, Monica, provides guidance in the dream by pointing to the balloons. Looking to her past might suggest ways for Nicole to be happy in the future.

Several of the dream's symbols point to positive qualities on which Nicole may want to focus. The girls exchange **Gifts**, an act of harmony, with the cuddly toy a sign of love and affection and the pirate hat hinting at play, with just a touch of adventure and law-breaking. **Yellow** can be a rather ambivalent shade, but in the dream it is a bright yellow and reflects in the girls' faces, so it probably stands for the sun, and therefore intuition, faith and goodness. **Orange**, particularly in India and the Far East, suggests spirituality, love and happiness.

Balls, and therefore **Balloons** (which are floating balls), are also solar symbols, and Nicole feels energized as she chases them. Anything that flies can also represent aspirations, hopes and dreams. Nicole captures the one balloon that has floated away from the bunch, suggesting a spirit of independence. Her view of the countryside as she drifts along may represent a new ability to see things more clearly and objectively. Her sense of disappointment as the dream ends is further evidence of its illuminating and uplifting quality.

A dream of flying or floating is one way the unconscious finds to reconnect with the intrinsic joy of being alive. Nicole's happy leaping and floating give her new views of the countryside — fresh perspectives that make it wrong to dismiss the dream too readily as merely wish-fulfilment or a flight from reality.

Myths & Legends

In the ancient Greek legend of Hero and Leander, Hero is a beautiful woman imprisoned by her jealous father in a tower on the eastern shore of the Hellespont (the straits separating Greece from Turkey). Her lover, Leander, who lives on the western shore, swims across the Hellespont every night to spend the hours of darkness secretly with her, and swims back each morning. To guide him on his swim, Hero lights a lantern in her window. One night a storm blows out the light, and, losing his way, Leander is drowned. In the morning Hero sees his body at the foot of her tower and throws herself down to die with her lover.

You might find this legend moving but unrealistic. No man could swim the Hellespont twice in 24 hours, night after night, and after a storm the body would not be likely to end up under the right window. Yet emotionally, as a tragic tale of the love between man and woman and the self-sacrifice of both, it makes sense. This is precisely the kind of emotional impact that dreams can have. They trace our deepest hopes, desires and fears, and in this way they can provide us with a helpful reflection of the private concerns that pervade our lives.

The fact that myths and legends have the power to resonate with us after so many years shows their close connection to the human psyche. In creating these stories their unknown authors revealed profound wisdom, and compiled, in a sense, the first psychology textbooks. A study of myths and legends is, therefore, one of the most useful approaches to dream interpretation. It can help us to see much deeper into the storyline of a dream, as well as to understand any archetypal figures we may encounter in Level Three dreams.

Struggles between parents and children play a major role in early Greek myths – in particular, the violence done by Cronos, one of the Titans, toward his father the sky god Uranos, and the battle for supremacy between the Titans and the Olympians, ending in the triumph of Zeus. Anyone seriously anxious about family tensions will find powerful analogies in these myths. More uplifting are the quests of Ulysses and Jason, and the *Metamorphoses*, narrated by Ovid, all showing the transforming power of love. Reading the myths of any culture is strongly recommended as a way to exercise the imagination and prepare it for broad-minded dream interpretation.

Wish-Fulfilment

The Victorian poet Robert Browning wrote, "Ah, but a man's reach should exceed his grasp, or what's a heaven for?" In other words, we should all aspire to something greater than ourselves. Sigmund Freud considered dreams as offering a form of wish-fulfilment, compensating us for the many disappointments or restrictions of real life. This view underplays the importance of dreams for self-understanding and self-development, but it is worth taking seriously, for wish-fulfilment is certainly an ingredient in many dreams.

Freud saw wish-fulfilment as driven largely by sexual energies, but Carl Jung rejected this "pan-sexualism", and drew attention instead to our higher-order energies — what might be called spiritual aspirations. The Buddha expressed these as the desire to be free from suffering and to attain the deathless state of Nirvana. Poetry, again, puts the matter eloquently. In the *Rubaiyat of Omar Khayyam*, the narrator wistfully imagines shaping the world to his wishes, saying to his beloved, "Ah love, if you and I and fate could but conspire/ To grasp this sorry scheme of things entire,/ Would not we shatter it to bits,/ And then remake it nearer to the heart's desire?"

When interpreting our dreams, we can sometimes find that they reveal wishes we did not know we had. In this way dreams can help us to recognize hidden longings, leaving the conscious mind to decide whether such longings are attainable — and, if so, whether it would be right to take the steps that attainment would require, or whether it would be better to leave them as fantasies. Even our fantasies, once brought to the light of day, can help us to understand more about ourselves.

They can sometimes, for example, explain a deep-seated unhappiness, the cause of which may have long puzzled us.

Since our dreams are usually beyond our control, enjoyable wish-fulfilment may sometimes be abruptly terminated by less pleasant dream events. We may be on the brink of receiving an award of some kind, only for the ceremony to be unexpectedly interrupted; or we may be at an enjoyable party, only to discover suddenly that we are inappropriately dressed. This deflating moment could well be an important part of a

dream's logic. For example, our unconscious mind might be telling us that our wishes have no intrinsic value, are wildly unrealistic, or are fraught with hidden dangers. Perhaps this is somewhat analogous to a cartoon notion of training your pet: you let the pet do what it wants to do, then demonstrate the consequences by punishing it.

The kinds of wish-fulfilment experienced at the three levels of dreaming (see pp.28–31) may be very different. Level One dreams tend to contain consciously remembered wishes that went ungratified during the day. Level Two dreams may reveal more enduring wishes, perhaps a longing for the freedom we felt as a child. Most ambitiously, Level Three dreams may express the wish to find our spiritual self or spiritual home, and to realize immortal longings.

It is not always easy, or useful, to separate wish-fulfilments from "dream pointers" – the symbolic scenarios that might suggest a way to resolve some crucial current issue in our lives. The pointer often enacts the solution it recommends, as in the case of Chloe in Workshop No. 16 (pp.116–117), who was shown the importance of rising above family disappointments. The resolution Chloe found by climbing a ladder to find liberation and contentment could, of course, be a case of wish-fulfilment, but even wish-fulfilment – as Freud made clear – can be instructive and help to point the dreamer in the right direction to alleviate their discontent.

CREATIVE VISUALIZATION

Although dreams may not show us *how* to achieve what we wish for, they can help us to tap into our innate potential. Creative visualization offers a technique to help us with this process. To ease physical aches and pains, for example, you might picture drawing in healing white light with each in-breath and sending it to the site of discomfort with each out-breath; or you could envisage yourself running freely and painlessly along a beautiful beach. To prepare for a job interview, you might imagine yourself strong and confident, answering all questions with skill and ease. Make the visualization detailed and vivid, and use it regularly. Hold it in your mind just before sleep. In time, it may start to appear in your dreams, with all the potential benefits this may bring.

Dream Workshop No. 16

The Dreamer

Chloe, 21, is a student at law school in New York, studying for her final examinations. Her parents live several hundreds of miles away, and Chloe feels that they are far more interested in the studies and social life of her younger sister, who is still at high school.

THE DREAM

Chloe is wearing a red-and-white summer dress but with winter boots, which are making her feel very hot and uncomfortable. She is in Central Park, New York. Workmen in overalls and hard hats are all around her, taking measurements with tape measures. One of them is measuring the distance between one tree and another. Another is up a ladder, measuring the length of leaves and twigs.

Her parents come and meet her — supposedly for a picnic, but they have forgotten to bring any food. "Not to worry — we'll find something," they say. Chloe wants to pick one of the delicious-looking peaches from the trees but she can't reach them, and her Dad tells her off for trying. "They're not yours to take!" he shouts again and again, getting louder and louder. Finally, unable to bear it any longer, Chloe covers her ears and runs up the ladder to escape.

When she reaches the top, the workman has mysteriously vanished. Much to her delight, there on top of the tree is a delicious spread of all sorts of fruit and cakes, so she climbs onto a branch, sits down and tucks in, feeling very contented that she has such a fantastic view over the park.

INTERPRETATION

A sense of confusion runs throughout this dream. Chloe wears a **Summer Dress**, which suggests lightness and pleasure, but below them she is wearing incongruous **Winter Boots**, which are hot and uncomfortable. They hint at an underlying heaviness that is preventing her from enjoying her surroundings.

The busy **Workmen** in the park convey a sense that Chloe cannot quite relax. They probably link to her concern about her impending university examinations. However, the workmen are wearing **Hard Hats**, which seem unnecessary here, and **Measuring** trees, twigs and leaves — a seemingly pointless task. These symbols may relate to the study of law, and hint that Chloe may have become frustrated with its procedures and obsessive attention to detail.

The main focus of Chloe's dissatisfaction, however, seems to be her relationship with her **Parents**. On the one hand, she seems to think that her parents have failed her. They have forgotten the promised picnic — food is often a symbol of the emotions and of emotional support. On the other hand, Chloe sees that they restrict her independence. Her father reacts with anger when she tries to take a peach for herself.

The conclusion to the dream offers Chloe a resolution. The **Ladder** symbolizes her means of escape. At the top of the tree, she finds delicious food and a fine view. Now that she has left home and lives so far away, she has the opportunity to be more emotionally self-reliant and should seize this.

*W*hen a dream ends happily, this often serves a double purpose: it can give us a sense of relief from our deep–seated personal probems; and it can also suggest, symbolically, possible ways to resolve our issues in waking life. Here the message for the dreamer is that she should nurture her independence and overcome her disappointment about the lack of family support.

The Surreal

Surrealism was a highly influential art movement born in the 1920s. Paintings by Salvador Dalí, Paul Delvaux, René Magritte and Giorgio de Chirico, and photographs by Man Ray, are marked by strange juxtapositions that challenge our view of art and of reality. People float in the air in suits and bowler hats; machines and other hard objects **flop over table edges like slices of bacon; light and shadow** flout the laws of physics; and weird distortions of scale suggest a parallel universe where earthly science no longer prevails. How like the dream world, you may be thinking.

The Surrealists had their antecedents centuries earlier in the art of Hieronymus Bosch and Francisco Goya, and later Odilon Redon, demonstrating that Surrealism is a universal tendency of mind — not every mind perhaps, but minds that will question their relationship with external and internal phenomena. Surrealism was defined by one of its founders, the French artist André Breton, as an attempt to reproduce the "true process of thought".

Of course, Surrealism has entered our conscious and unconscious mind and may well have profoundly influenced the way we think. If so, this is likely to have been a two-way process: a receptiveness to Surrealist art is almost certainly due to its resonance with some deep-seated aspect of our imagination.

Dreams create their own mix of the relevant and the irrelevant, a **mental meandering in all directions, where memories, wishes and anxieties** acquire tangible form in a jumble of narrative and imagery. When Surrealism occurs in dreams, it takes us even further in the direction of the irrational — even, we may sometimes think, toward complete anarchy.

Surrealistic images are vivid and often **unforgettable** — most likely because they show the dreaming unconscious strongly impacting upon the waking mind. Does the unconscious, therefore, use memorable, Surrealist imagery because it has an especially urgent message to impart? Perhaps, sometimes. But there is no need for anyone to be overly concerned by a surreal dream: it is simply one of the many devices used by the unconscious to convey a particular message or series of messages to the dreamer.

Surreal dreams remind us of the imagination's innate creative resources, and often make us yearn for vivid artistic experiences, as creator or as recipient. These are the dreams that we are most likely to write down and to describe to people during the day. Jung claimed that we all dream 24 hours a day, but the dream world is filtered out by the conscious mind during waking hours. In sleep deprivation experiments, and in certain physical conditions such as mild epilepsy, the individual can be simultaneously aware of both being awake and dreaming, and it seems likely that through practices such as meditation, which calms the conscious mind,

we could all train ourselves to experience this. As mentioned before, Dalí, most celebrated of the Surrealists, deliberately held his mind in the hypnagogic state, between waking and sleeping, so that he could use in his paintings the images that presented themselves in this halfway house of awareness. The results have an almost magical ability to create a subtle shift in our consciousness. As in dreams, Dalí allows each image in his paintings to represent several things at once, to remind us of the many possible meanings of each aspect of our experience. A sea shell is also an eye, a fruit bowl is also a girl's nose and forehead. Objects metamorphose into each other or behave in uncharacteristic ways. Rules no longer apply, and it is as if the dreaming mind is projected directly onto the canvas.

Like dreams, Surrealism reminds us that **things are not always what they seem: reality is fluid, rather than static.** Surrealist works of art makes "sense" to us because we recognize them from our dreams: we have been there. And these works express the same underlying wish as our dreams — that the waking world would not mislead us into believing only a partial view of reality.

Dream Workshop No. 17

The Dreamer

Jenny, 35, is a nurse who has just been accepted on a course of training to become a midwife. She is divorced, with no children, and is looking for romance. She would like to start a family and is anxious about her biological clock ticking away.

THE DREAM

In a desert landscape there are tiny kangaroos leaping all around. Jenny feels lonely and is frightened of the kangaroos. Someone unseen speaks the word "Rat" out loud, which startles her. A tree emerges from the sand, and starts to put out leaves. But the leaves turn into books, full of algebraic equations and foreign languages that look like Arabic and Hebrew. One of the tiny kangaroos comes right up to Jenny and asks, in English, whether she might have some sandwiches to spare. When she answers "No", the kangaroo does not understand. But Jenny then plucks one of the books from the tree, and the first page she looks at tells her to search inside her pocket. There she finds a sandwich she had forgotten about, and hands it to the kangaroo. She feels less lonely. She looks at the books' pages fluttering in the breeze, and thinks how beautiful they are.

INTERPRETATION

The dream seems accurately to reflect Jenny's present situation. The **Desert** landscape is an obvious symbol of emotional isolation and of barrenness. At 35 she is concerned that the possibilities for motherhood are declining as the years go by.

The **Kangaroos** are an interesting symbol, which may refer to motherhood — a kangaroo carries the newborn in her body even after it has left the womb. Jenny might find it helpful to examine the fear that the tiny kangaroos aroused in her. This may stem from her anxiety over the fact that she does not yet have children. Or is some other matter troubling her?

The word "**Rat**" also needs more thought. It could be linked to feelings of anger about herself or her ex-husband over the marriage and divorce, which have left her childless. But it may also refer to something else. Perhaps only work with word association will enable her to arrive at the meaning; the unseen person who utters the word could perhaps be identified in the same way.

On a happier note, a **Tree** is a symbol of fertility and also of inner development and unfolding. In this case the leaves that turn into books may relate to Jenny's future studies as a midwife. Even though the books are written in **Foreign Languages**, which she does not yet understand, she succeeds in reading one of the pages, implying that she knows more than she thinks she does.

The dream ends positively. The beauty of the pages fluttering in the wind may be a sign that she will find satisfaction in learning, or it may suggest the possibilities for new relationships that this chapter in her life may offer. The **Pocket** could symbolize her womb. Feeding the kangaroo helps her to feel less lonely: the **Sandwich** she finds may imply that she has access to hidden sources of emotional nourishment and thus has more to offer children than she has so far realized.

*T*he most enjoyable dreams are often both surreal and eclectic.
Rich in imagery, this example works by suggestion rather than by
clear narrative: the dreamer is anxious about being childless, and the tiny
kangaroos reflect her worries through fascinating ambiguity.

Thinking & Dreaming

Developing skills in dream recall and dream interpretation helps us to explore and to understand the processes that go on within our own minds. Without work such as this, the operation of the unconscious may remain a mystery to us.

There is an illuminating analogy with meditation here. Meditation trains us to observe and, to some extent, control what is going on in our minds. By focusing on something simple, such as breathing, the meditator avoids being distracted by the stream of thoughts that usually dominate awareness. As the meditator's skills become more advanced, he or she is able to focus attention on these thoughts while remaining detached from them, as if the thoughts were an objective rather than a subjective phenomenon. This enables the meditator to explore the nature and manner of thought and of the emotions connected with thought.

Dream intepretation is most effective when a similar state of detached alertness can be achieved. This helps us to analyze what was happening in our mind during the course of a dream. For example, we might ask ourselves: What was I thinking when this or that occurred? What was I feeling? Why did I act as I did? And so on. If we obtain a picture of how our minds function in dreams, when the unconscious is in control, we can begin to understand how our unconscious influences our thoughts and actions in waking life. For it is a mistake to suppose that, even when we are awake, it is our conscious minds that run our lives for us.

Working on dreams in this way also gives us a good appreciation of the differences between dream logic and waking logic. In waking life we are aware of cause and effect: if I close the curtains, the room will be darker. But in dreams effects frequently have no observable cause — the light may suddenly grow dim for no apparent reason. We often find ourselves in dream situations with no idea how or why they came about.

In his research Jung drew attention to a phenomenon that he called synchronicity — the fact that, in both waking life and in dreams, our minds often link things together not by cause and effect but by meaning. For example, we have a sudden, unexpected thought that a friend is in trouble, and the next moment she rings to tell us so. The one event did not cause the other, yet the two are closely related. In dreams the more attentively we observe events, the more we see that synchronicity, rather than cause and effect, is involved. And the more we become conscious of synchronicity in dreams, the more we become conscious of it in waking life. In some people this heightened sensitivity acquired through dream work leads to an increase in synchronous experiences.

Becoming atttuned to the strange logic of dreams also enables us to recognize some of their other vagaries. We may find, for example, that although dreams are not bound by the laws of waking life, some things still turn out to be impossible. We may be unable to walk through walls or on water, try though we might. We may even lose some of our real-life abilities in dreams — perhaps certain mental accomplishments (such as simple arithmetic), or the senses of taste and touch, or skills such as singing or whistling.

Detaching yourself from your dream during intepretation, just as the meditator detaches himself or herself from thoughts and emotions, is a good basis for getting to the heart of such mysteries. Inevitably, the reasons for these various checks on dream occurences will differ from dreamer to dreamer, and may convey important messages.

The inability to walk through walls, for example, could symbolize some obstructions that we are unwittingly putting in our own way. Being unable to walk on water could relate to a fear of self-exposure. Detachment gives us the power to concentrate fully, and be alert to every aspect of detail and mood in a dream, and see how these things relate to any issues that are affecting our lives. Only then will we be able to make the right connections to arrive at a reliable interpretation.

Many people cocoon themselves in an unrealistic self-image, unable even to acknowledge the problems they face, never mind start to solve them. Working with dreams can be helpful in the process of moving from degrees of self-delusion to heightened self-awareness. However, it is important to *want* to achieve this fresh vision of the self. For those who are reluctant to open up to self-scrutiny, the best encouragement is to think of the satisfaction that perception, rather than unawareness, brings. It is like the difference between tap water and spring water: tap water is a perfectly pleasant way to quench our thirst until we have tasted the purity of a mountain spring.

Recurring Dreams

Recurring dreams, in which the same scenario appears **again and again**, are among the most interesting of our dream experiences. So too are dreams in which the same themes keep reappearing, but with different details. One such theme in my own dreams has to do with trains, though trains are not a particular interest of mine in waking life. Sometimes the carriages are crowded and I can't find a seat; at other times they are almost empty. Sometimes the interiors are rich, with plush decor in reds and golds, while at other times they are austere and shabby. Sometimes I catch or leave the trains at stations I knew as a boy, but then sometimes the stations are unfamiliar. While the context varies, all these dreams follow the main theme of travelling, which, of course, relates to the idea of progressing in life.

Recurring dreams are often relatively short and uncomplicated, yet they can provide some of the most rewarding material for interpretation. Typical examples would be **a dream of being pursued through dark streets** by a pack of dogs, of horses galloping across a meadow, or of talking to a stranger whose face is hidden. Recurring dreams tend to carry a strong emotional charge. Anxiety or fear is typical, but sometimes the feeling can be positive, giving a sense of reassurance that can persist for days. Some people report frustration that the dream keeps returning. It may come at intervals of weeks, months, even years, yet it is always instantly recognized.

When interpreting recurring dreams (direct association tends to work well; see p.50), it is important to persist until an idea resonates strongly and leads to a possible interpretation. If the dream does not recur after this, you have probably found the correct interpretation, but if it continues, more work is needed. However, with recurring dreams that produce a positive emotional response – as may happen with Level Three dreams – detailed interpretation may be unnecessary. The purpose of the **dream may be to convey some mystical truth** that cannot be reduced to words.

Rather different are recurring "false awakenings", in which the dreamer may be so sure of being awake that they then dream of getting out of bed and going downstairs. Dreams such as these seem to demonstrate that the difference between dreaming and wakefulness is less clear than we suppose.

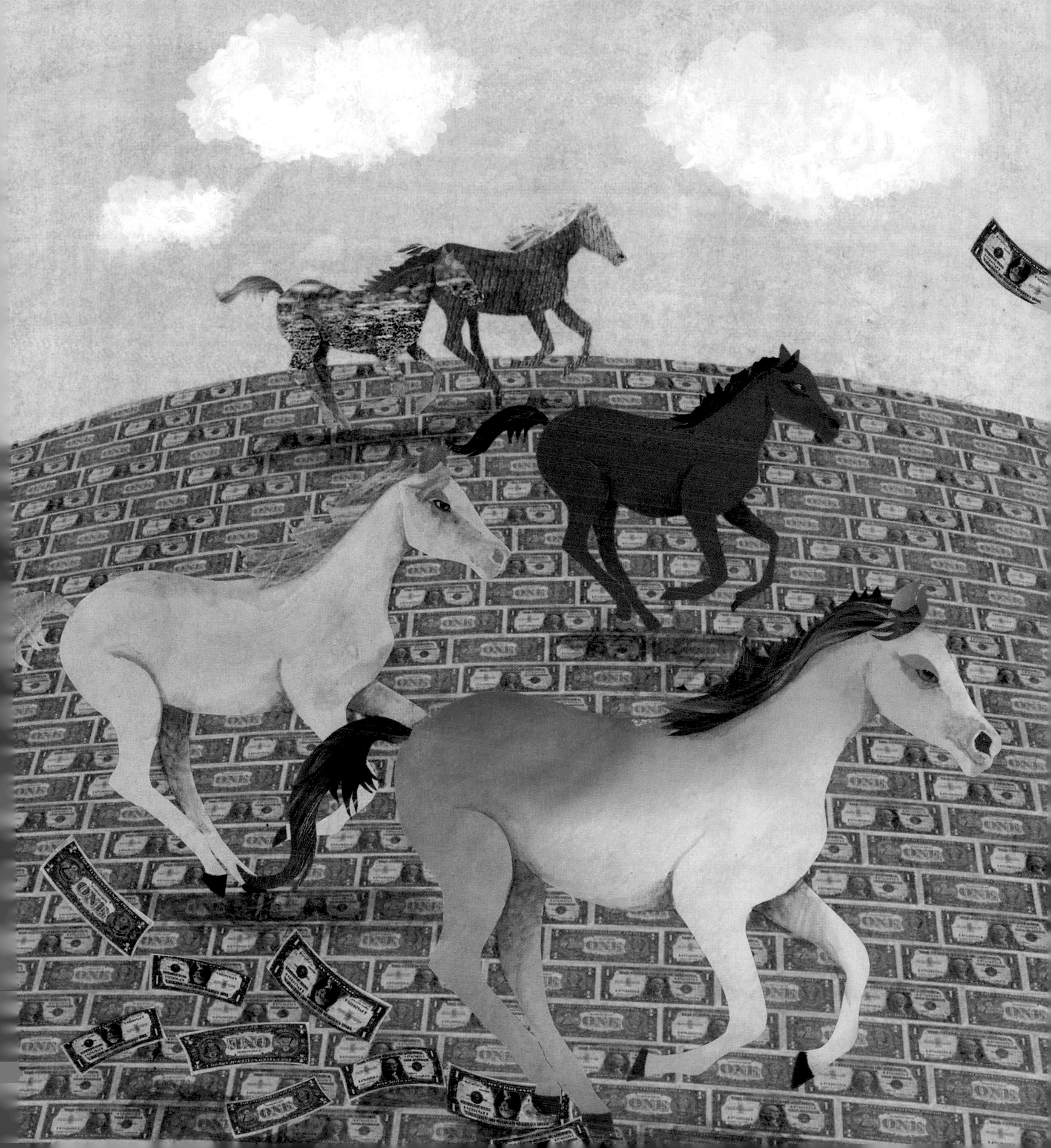

Dream Emotions

Emotions do not behave logically even in waking life. It is not uncommon to say, for example, "I don't know why I felt like that," or "I lost it for a moment." Emotions often seem to control us rather than the other way round. Nevertheless, although their strength or even their character may take us by surprise, we can usually see what prompted them. In simple situations it is easy to link cause and effect: we receive good news and our spirits rise, we walk in the country and become relaxed, we see a sad movie and find ourselves moved to tears.

In dreams this obvious link between cause and effect is sometimes lost. We might find ourselves unmoved by extreme violence, yet saddened by a light shower of rain; we might feel joy at finding an old book on a dusty shelf, yet be indifferent on being handed a suitcase full of banknotes.

Dream emotions can be as strong as waking ones: their intensity can still be with us when we wake up, with the result that we can be left in high spirits or in deep gloom. They are often much more childlike than waking feelings. As children our emotional range is limited by our narrow understanding: a broken toy can cause us

grief, while news of an earthquake in Peru will mean little. Adult dreams at Levels One and Two can recapture something of this innocence. We can seem to face the events depicted in much the same way that we faced real events in childhood.

Nevertheless, by paying attention to our dream emotions, we can learn a lot about what motivates or unsettles us as individuals. The "logic" of these emotions is that they are the natural — even selfish — responses of a child, unaffected by custom and conditioning.

Compare this with the sense we have in our everyday lives that we *ought* to respond to things in certain ways. So often, we are influenced by the emotions of others: if everyone around us is crying, we feel like crying too. (This tendency to empathize appears to be innate, as even very young children will start to cry if they see another child in tears.) Humans are social animals, and our emotions in waking life are, in part, social responses.

Yet however socially active we are in waking life, in dreams we dream alone, so our feelings arise spontaneously. This can help to draw our attention to the things that really affect us at an emotional level. Often these are

Tears for your
sake or for theirs?

small, intimate things — the loss of a comb, the discovery that a friend has stolen your seat on a train or, more positively, being rewarded for having the cleanest shoes. Such incidents can stand in for a whole range of deep-rooted feelings. Particularly common are the many shades of feeling associated with being hurt or frustrated — jealousy, resentment, envy. We know in waking life that these emotions are unworthy of us, and often fail to acknowledge them. So the dream can help us by revealing the degree to which we are motivated by embarrassing personal emotions rather than the shared values we are expected to feel — self-confidence, solidarity, compassion. In dreams, instead of being the emotional clone of others, we discover ourselves in all our frailties — provided that we can read the symbolism and mood of a dream with imagination and honesty.

One approach to dream emotions, then, is to use them for self-discovery, through intepretation. But there is another possible approach, which many people might prefer. Dream emotions are arguably more controllable than those of waking life, so instead of self-revelation we can use the dream world as a kind of psychic tonic.

The more we work with the dream world, the more it becomes responsive to our wishes. Thus the simple strategy of affirming to ourselves before we go to sleep that we will have pleasant, happy dreams and wake in good spirits next morning can have a marked effect on dream content. We may start to experience contentment, joy and self-realization in our dreams — and perhaps, occasionally, the profound depths of Level Three. This in turn can work subtle changes in the unconscious. Dreams are our friends, and if we have a seemingly fragmented and stressful dream life, it may be partly because we have been failing to benefit from their friendship.

Dream Workshop No. 18

The Dreamer

Jane, 44, a successful financier has recently been exploring yoga and meditation, and has started taking classes on Buddhism. She has also decided to give a portion of her income to a child poverty relief charity.

THE DREAM

Jane is standing on a cliff top, looking down at a white-and-red-striped lighthouse out on a tiny rock. It's daylight, but the lighthouse is still throwing out its beam in a regular pulse. The sea is very stormy, and there are fishing boats that look as if they are about to capsize. But on the cliff top it feels perfectly calm and still — there's no wind. Jane notices that the fishermen have umbrellas up, and some of the boats even have umbrellas for sails. She puts out her hand to see if it's raining where she is. It isn't, and she wonders why. A little bird lands on her outstretched palm and starts to swivel around like a mechanical bird, singing, "Today, today. Today's the day." Then Jane is standing in front of a white temple. She senses that her great aunt (who died eight years ago) will be waiting for her inside.

INTERPRETATION

Jane's newfound interests may have suggested much of the symbolism in this dream. The calm that Jane finds on the **Cliff Top** may be affirming the peace she finds in meditation. The meditator is above the confused sea of thoughts that characterize the conscious mind, and abides at another level of being. The **Stormy Seas** may represent the perils and challenges of everyday life.

The **Lighthouse Beam** may link to Buddhism, which lays great emphasis on the "clear light" of ultimate reality. This light is seen just after death and offers the individual the opportunity to experience enlightenment and escape the cycle of future rebirth and death.

Jane may also be aware that in Buddhism **Red** symbolizes life, while **White** stands for redemption and transformation. A **Bird** is one of the symbols of the Buddha, while the **Umbrella** stands for protection and for Nirvana. This array of Buddhist symbols may simply suggest that Jane's mind is re-examining what it has recently learnt. However, Jane would be justified in also seeing them as signs of support and encouragement for her in her chosen path.

The white **Temple** reinforces the spiritual meaning, even though there is nothing to suggest that it is specifically Buddhist. Jane may find the answers she is looking for by further exploring her spirituality. The expectation that her **Deceased Great-Aunt** will be waiting for her inside the temple is fascinatingly mysterious. The aunt may symbolize the welcome that awaits the believer in the afterlife. Or if Jane had a special relationship with this aunt, perhaps there could be an element of wish-fulfilment at work?

The reference to "**Today**" is important: Buddhism and meditation emphasize the importance of being in the moment, rather than distracted by memories, or worries about the past or the future. Is this a message that while spirituality is of great value, Jane should not forget to enjoy life on Earth as well?

*W*hen someone you love who has died appears in a dream, without causing any renewed feelings of grief, this could be a sign that you are ready to accept their death, while giving them due thanks for what they contributed to your life. Living in the moment, as the bird urges, means acknowledging the past for what it is — immensely valuable but not a place to remain in.

Multi-layered Dreams

Dr. Calvin Hall, the leading dream researcher and expert on personality theory, identified five levels at which we try to organize our inner and outer reality. In summary these are:

1. *The way in which we see ourselves (our self-concepts).*
2. *The way in which we see others (our concepts about other people).*
3. *The way in which we see the world (our concepts about values and our physical environment).*
4. *The way in which we see our motives and impulses, and the methods by which we realize the former and control the latter.*
5. *The way in which we conceptualize our inner conflicts and our attempts to solve them.*

Dr. Hall subdivided the last of these into: conflicts with parents during the struggle for independence and the process of distinguishing parental feelings from our own (desire for security versus desire for freedom); conflicts over our sex roles; the conflict between our own impulses and the constraints imposed by society; and the conflict between life and death, creativity and destruction. Hall concluded that dreams reflect the way in which the mind tries to understand these different conflicts and attempts, consciously and unconsciously, to resolve them.

Other research suggests that the purposes of dreams are not so easily summarized. They cannot be reduced to attempts to formulate a set of morals and values — just as they refuse to be straitjacketed by the Freudian theory of them as wish-fulfilments arising from sexual instincts and repressions. Hall's work draws useful attention to the influence that inner conflicts may have on our dreams and on the multi-layered meanings behind them.

For example, you have a dream in which you are trying to tidy a room, only to find that when you thought you had finished, it looks just as messy. You eventually abandon your efforts and live in the room as it is. Dream interpretation might initially suggest

that this has to do with the conflict of trying to please your parents in your youth, or perhaps even in later life, while preferring to go your own way. But if you look at the dream again, it may also symbolize a confusion of self-concepts. Are you really obedient or are you anarchic? Do you prefer security or freedom? The answers are not obvious. Consider the dream a third time and it may suggest a breaking of rules, and thus the conflict between impulsiveness and control, or sexual freedom and restraint. Viewed in a different light again, it may suggest a tension between creativity and destructiveness — and thus ultimately between life and death.

Any one of these interpretations may satisfy, but we may also recognize a connection between them: that the dream is really about all the many conflicting pressures and desires of everyday life, and discovering who we are among them.

This is primarily a Level Two dream, but, as discussed in Chapter I, dreams can sometimes combine all three levels, starting at Level One and going progressively deeper, culminating in Level Three. This demonstrates the interrelated nature of the various levels of the unconscious. A holistic view of dreams is that, like kaleidoscopic mirrors, they are able to show the many facets of the whole self.

Working with dreams brings about an improved communication between the unconscious and conscious minds, helping us to remember recent dreams, but also to access dreams from the more distant past. Dream memories may arise spontaneously during the day, prompted by events that seem to be connected with them or even, puzzlingly, to have been predicted by them. A point may also be reached where the mind can rove with increasing freedom through its inner dream diary. Among the many significant discoveries that usually follow from this is that the unconscious stores even long-forgotten dreams — perhaps reflecting their importance to our mental, emotional and spiritual life. That these are true memories of our own dreams is unmistakable: dream memories carry an inimitable character of their origin deep in our psyches, which is recognized by the fully alert conscious. We understand ourselves better than we know.

Dream Workshop No. 19

The Dreamer

Teresa, 47, is a freelance writer who earns her living writing articles for women's magazines. A single mother with two young children, she feels frustrated by financial and family pressures, and wishes that she could spend more time writing the novel she knows is inside her.

THE DREAM

Teresa finds herself in an empty red room with a wooden floor — a dining room. There is a wooden table in the room, with chairs that seem to have been waiting for years for someone to sit on them. Above the table hangs a white clock, shaped like a flower. Stephanie, an old friend, comes into the room and Teresa takes the clock off the wall and shows it to her. Stephanie admires it, but only hurriedly, as she has to rush off elsewhere. Teresa is disappointed. Then she sees that the room has changed from red to dark blue. Suddenly, she notices a silver stepladder, which she tentatively climbs, worrying all the time that she may fall off. As she nears the top, she does indeed fall, but to her amazement she bounces off the floor like a ball, up to the ceiling, then down again … up and down, many times. Bouncing in slow motion, she feels exhilarated.

INTERPRETATION

A **Dining Room** can symbolize a dreamer's social life and the idea of sharing, but this room is empty, perhaps suggesting Teresa's loneliness. The neglected chairs may also represent the characters in the novel she hopes to write, who still wait to be created.

Red can represent energy and extroverted emotions. Although **Wood** can stand for integrity and dependability, it can also represent constraint — a "wooden" approach to life. All this strengthens our impression that Teresa's desire for a more satisfying emotional life is currently frustrated. Perhaps she wishes to reach out to an audience of readers, as well as enlarge her circle of friends.

The **Flower-shaped Clock** relates to Teresa's talents as a writer. But time is passing while the flower of creativity remains unopened. Stephanie's reaction hints that, in Teresa's opinion, her friends are not giving her the encouragement she needs.

The dream changes abruptly, which may indicate that it is actually two dreams in one. The walls change to **Dark Blue** — perhaps the "blues" of disappointment. **Silver** is a symbol for the moon, magic and inspiration, and the **Stepladder**, which Teresa climbs despite her fears, suggests that she should take more risks with her creative life: she **Falls** but then **Bounces** back up.

The dream seems to tell her not to be discouraged if creative success does not come at once. Or perhaps the joyful bouncing is a liberated form of creativity: she may find satisfaction by using her talents playfully rather than in solemn earnest. This might not in the short term bring friendship: a writer's lot can be a lonely one. But who knows about the longer term? The bouncing may also encourage her to play more with her children while they are young — although interestingly, they do not appear in the dream.

*D*reams can reflect a number of different dissatisfactions simultaneously,
through multi-layering. Here the dreamer feels both alone (she is a single parent and
her opportunities for socializing are limited) and frustrated in her creativity.
The dream hints that taking risks might bring more satisfaction within her reach.

5

Guide to Dream Themes

People sometimes complain that they dream about inconsequential things, rather than the topics that really interest them. However, as you begin to understand the language of dreams, you'll see that they do, in fact, touch on the central concerns in our lives — time, morality, discovery, love, loss, and various fears and desires. Interpretation can yield illuminating insights into key themes.

Introduction to Dream Themes

Thanks to the work of dream researchers such as Dr. Calvin Hall and Robert Van de Castle, we have a wealth of information about the most commonly occurring symbols in our dream lives. The great dream interpreters have also given us thought-provoking ideas about what these symbols might signify. When we talk of dream themes, this is what we tend to mean — not the images themselves but their underlying meaning.

For example, a common theme in your dreams might be communication — perhaps because you encounter obstacles in your attempts to express yourself to some people, perhaps because your partner tends to be uncommunicative. In the former case, the problem could also be expressed as low self-esteem, which often prevents people from talking openly about themselves. In the latter case, the problem could be restated, more broadly, as being about relationships. Communication only works well if there is a healthy level of both expressiveness and responsiveness, and there are many possible reasons for it to break down.

We know from other studies that the mind, particularly in the young, can turn frequently to thoughts of a sexual nature.

Why, then, does this theme not feature as a main category in Hall's list of common dream motifs (see pp.38-39)? To answer this, we need to bear in mind that Hall's classification is based on surface content: if a sexual dream features not kissing or copulation but, say, a phallic train entering a dark tunnel, it would be categorized by Hall under "conveyances", rather than sex.

Overtly sexual dreams do occur, of course, but not as often as we might expect. Disguised sexual dreams seem to strengthen Sigmund Freud's view that erotic impulses tend to be expressed in symbols, perhaps to avoid rousing the conscious mind from sleep by their outrageous nature. An alternative possibility is that Freud was incorrect and that, except in instances of extreme repression, the unconscious has little need to dream about sex, since the conscious mind is well able to engage in sexual fantasies as often as it pleases while awake. It is also interesting that during adolescence — a time of intense sexual awakening — there is less attempt by the unconscious to disguise the true meaning of its dreams, even those that are openly sexual, perhaps because nature is testing that the sexual response is working effectively.

Level Two dreams are very much about who we are and who we want to be — so the theme of self-image becomes paramount. Often intriguing, sometimes saturated with nostalgic longing or wistful fantasy, dreams at this level reveal more of the richness and complexity of our identities than do the more superficial Level One dreams. Interpretation can take us far beyond the ostensible symbolic content, and at a certain point we may find ourselves working with inner anxieties and appetites that are only tenuously connected with the dream itself. However, this hardly matters: exploring tenuous connections — especially those between the symbols and our inner selves — is the whole point of interpretation, and can be a springboard to enhanced self-awareness.

Level Three dreams are more concerned with grand themes. Often of a seemingly spiritual nature, they appear to reveal deep secrets, revelations that become clear to us while dreaming, but then just elude the conscious mind on waking. The *lingua franca* of these dreams is archetypal figures and symbols (see pp.21–25), beautiful landscapes, far horizons, and vistas of peace and abundance. The underlying themes often appear elusive and ineffable because they operate on a plane far beyond our usual understanding. They are resistant to language — sometimes even to poetry. Although these Level Three dreams usually have a gentle, loving quality, they can sometimes be challenging, even disturbing. We may feel as if we are being questioned or judged in some way, as if the book of our lives has been opened, revealing our failures and shortcomings. We may feel we are in the presence of a stern, but just, guardian or parent, who cares for us but wishes us to confront who we are and who we might be. Level Three dreams can be life-changing, leaving us feeling we have accessed deeper levels of ourselves — even somehow participated more intimately in the spirit.

We can often train ourselves to dream certain themes. One way is to tell yourself during the day that you will dream of the desired theme that night, then hold it in your mind as you drift off to sleep. The theme may relate to general issues, or particular people. Try looking at a photograph of the person in question, or someone who embodies your chosen dream theme in some way, before you sleep. You may then dream of them, but often not in ways you might expect.

Dream Workshop No. 20

The Dreamer

Lucy, 55, has just been made redundant after 15 years as an administrative assistant. She hasn't enjoyed her work for years, but she is looking for another job in the same area. Nothing has materialized yet and she's starting to worry about money.

THE DREAM

It's high summer, but Lucy has been busy inside, cleaning her house with the shades down – she feels that the bright sunlight would distract her. Other people have been helping – a girl called Sally, with whom she used to work, and Mr Anderson, who gave her a job in a florist's when she was 14. (In reality, she has had no contact with these people in years.) Their main task has been to pin down the letters, bills and other papers that have been escaping from the office and flying about the house, by putting stones on top of them. But Lucy has also been sweeping away a lot of cobwebs from the ceiling. As she deals with the last one, she realizes that the lovely little spider that was in it has landed on her hand, so she runs outside and places it on one of the red flowers in her well-kept garden.

She feels very relieved to be outside, so takes a deep breath and bends over to hug her white tulips. They turn pink and come away in her arms. As she stands up, still holding them, she sees that a whole new set of flowers has already regrown in the soil. The papers are now starting to fly out of the front door, some with cobwebs hanging from them, but this no longer disturbs Lucy. She's happy: her flowers are filling her with joy.

INTERPRETATION

The image of **Cleaning the House** in Lucy's dream suggest her desire for change, though her efforts to keep out the light may also indicate that she fears taking risks. She is helped by **Former Acquaintances**, implying that she could call upon past experiences in her attempt to change her life. She might think back not only to the florist's helpfulness but perhaps also to the ambitions she had for herself in those distant days.

The **Papers** flying about the house seem an obvious symbol for her dissatisfaction with her career to date and may also symbolize banknotes. Weighing them down with stones perhaps suggests that Lucy wishes to "bury" this part of her life and the anxieties associated with it.

Cobwebs reinforce the idea that Lucy felt "trapped" by her career. However, in freeing herself from the cobwebs, she also frees the beautiful spider, causing her to run outside. Does this indicate that there were some good things about the past after all? Lucy should consider more closely how various past experiences may help to guide her in her choice of a new career.

Flowers are prominent in the dream, representing creativity and new life. When Lucy embraces her tulips, they flush **Pink**, with a sudden infusion of vitality. Although she gathers them in her arms, more grow in their place – metaphorically, perhaps she need not be afraid of uprooting heself? Finally, the papers and cobwebs fly out of the house – they are no longer relevant to Lucy's life. Can she make a creative new start, and turn her back on tedious administrative work for ever?

Old acquaintances appearing in a dream may imply a general reference to an earlier time of life. It is always worth asking in such cases what you have learned from the past and what it can still teach you. Have you neglected any of its potential lessons? Here, old acquaintances prompt an overdue reassessment for a dreamer in her fifties.

Fear & Anxiety

Physiological measurements have shown that fear and anxiety are felt by all higher animals: they are survival instincts, gearing us up for the "fight or flight" response. But humans are probably alone in feeling anxieties that stem from their imagination. We often worry about things that might go wrong in our personal or professional lives. And our knowledge of our inevitable mortality is a potent cause of fear, not only triggered by the prospect of our own death, but also by **the thought of all the dangers that surround ourselves and our loved ones every day.** Yet while dreams of death can be disturbing and upsetting, often they reflect some other kind of change in waking life, perhaps leaving a job or ending a relationship.

... at the wheel of a car but I couldn't reach the brakes and ...

It is easy, then, to see why anxiety dreams loom so large in many people's experience. Work is a common source of worry, for it is here that our performance is subject to the most explicit kind of review, and where potentially we can be responsible for massive amounts of money and for the well-being and safety of lots of other people. Work anxiety can lead, for example, to dreams involving a fear of falling, readily interpreted as concern that there is no secure foundation to our position. A person may try to hide their fears with overwork or attempts

... my teeth started to fall out and crumble one by one, filling up ...

at nonchalance, but the unconscious is not deceived. Dreams can help us to conduct our own job performance appraisal and point us to the need, in addition, to address the life-work balance when job pressures start to get out of hand.

When we fall in love or have children, **we create hostages to fortune. Our fears are no longer for ourselves but for those dear to us.** We might dream of struggling to rescue our loved ones from drowning or abduction — news coverage of the latter in real life gives our unconscious rich material. New parents commonly dream that they roll over onto the baby in their sleep. Parenting worries (due to lack of confidence in our skills or guilt over various kinds of imagined neglect) are most often characterized in dreams by concerns for a child's safety.

... trying to run away from him but my legs just wouldn't move ...

Past fears can also make our dreams anxious, reflecting underlying issues with self-esteem that continue into the present. A classic example is the dream that **we have failed to prepare for an exam.** It is as if the unconscious has reached back into our inner history for an analogy we will understand.

Anxiety dreams can also reflect post-traumatic stress. The body tries to dissipate the nervous disturbances it still feels by expressing them, in the same way that talking about a bad experience can be therapeutic.

Unknown?
Unfulfilment?
Future?
Loneliness?
Homelessness?

Empty space

Heights

Responsibility?
Exposure?
Immobility?
Risk?
Temptation?

Panic?
Worry?
Doom?
Inevitability?
Compulsion?

Mood cues

Dream Workshop No. 21

The Dreamer

Kerry, 34, works as a translator and has been living in Paris for 10 years, having moved from Boston. Her mother and family, including her grandmother, still live in Boston, so she doesn't see them as often as she'd like. However, when she does visit them, she always finds returning to Paris emotionally draining, despite loving her life there.

THE DREAM

Kerry is in a theatre. There is a slim female dancer on stage, in a long, vibrant pink dress. The spotlight is shining down on her, and Kerry is watching from one of the theatre's boxes, with her grandmother beside her. They have a great view, and Kerry feels lucky to have secured these seats. However, despite being inside, she feels that it might start raining on them at any moment and doesn't want her grandmother to get cold.

A young man in a sailor's uniform is also in the box with them. She doesn't know who he is and wonders why he's there. He leans over and whispers affectionately, "You next." Kerry is not sure what he means, but she starts to panic as she doesn't know the dance, so wouldn't be able to perform in front of all these people. Her grandmother senses her worry and strokes her hair reassuringly, saying it doesn't matter if it rains.

INTERPRETATION

The key to understanding this dream is its setting. The **Theatre** is well known as a symbol of life itself, and Kerry's appreciation of their good seats and "great view" indicate that she takes a healthy interest in things. She enjoys observing the success of others, in this case a dancer – someone who moves across the stage with ease.

However, Kerry is much less secure in the role of performer. She panics when it seems that she will be the next person on display. She doesn't want to be under the **Spotlight** – the object of attention. She is made aware of skills she does not possess, rather than her strengths. Perhaps Kerry would find it helpful to look more closely at the reasons for her lack of self-confidence.

The **Sailor** is interesting. A young sailor is often a symbol for adventure, so this seems to suggest that Kerry does have a bolder side. He implies "affectionately" that things are expected of her. Perhaps if she draws on her courage and throws herself into the performance, she will be a success.

The **Rain** that Kerry fears will fall even though she and her grandmother are inside the protective shell of the theatre hints at a general feeling of apprehension – even when enjoying comfort and security in life, she fears that she is still not safe from misfortune.

Her **Grandmother** could symbolize Kerry's own frailer and more vulnerable self, which she worries will feel the **Cold** if ever misfortune should occur. This may represent emotional cold – the loss of love. However, even this more vulnerable side of herself offers reassurance, stroking her hair – an action we often use to comfort a child – and telling her that it doesn't matter if it rains. She will be able to handle it. The dream's message may be that, despite Kerry's vulnerable side, she is resilient and able to withstand pressure.

*O*ther characters in a dream may often represent various (maybe contradictory) aspects of ourselves — like the grandmother and sailor here. This can be true even when a dream character — such as a grandmother — is a person actually known to the dreamer. Simultaneously, though, she remains the grandmother — someone the dreamer loves and wishes to protect.

Relationships

Relationships have the potential to be profoundly nourishing — even when they have destructive elements in them, as they so often do. By understanding our relationships better, we can eliminate the negative and emphasize the positive. Dreams can help us with this alchemy.

From the moment of conception, we live much of our lives in the context of other people. Early relationships with parents and teachers provide us with most of our education; and, even in later years, our state of mind will reflect the ways in which they and others treated us in childhood. Crucially, our sense of who we are is in large measure conditioned by what others tell us about ourselves, by the extent to which they value us, and by the amount of emotional autonomy they allow us to have.

It follows naturally that relationships play a significant role in our dreams. Paradoxically, we often find that we dream as much about people we hardly know, or about complete strangers, as about those close to us. Sometimes the characters we encounter seem to be figments of our dreaming imagination. But a caveat is necessary: even dreams that appear to be about people from whom we are quite distant can in fact have something illuminating to tell us about our most cherished relationships.

If we have no repressed emotions toward our intimates, and can express ourselves freely to them in waking life, we are fortunate.

It would be unwise, however, to assume that many of us are in this position. Even the happiest relationships have issues, often unacknowledged by the people involved, even privately.

There is a difference between issues and insecurities, both of which are likely to surface in dreams. An issue is a point of tension that is woven into the texture of the relationship, often involving differences of temperament or attitude. Communication issues can play a part in dreams about relationships, because the tensions involved often hinder the ability of two people to have an open dialogue. Any dream involving flawed communication — perhaps a cell phone turning into a hamburger just as you start to speak — may be prompted by problems that have never been properly discussed between you and another person in your life.

Whereas issues are two-sided, insecurities tend to be experienced by just one party to a relationship. You might worry that you are unworthy of a friendship, that your partner will leave you for someone else, or that you are unable to provide the financial or emotional support they need. There may or may not be good reasons for such feelings. Many insecurities are groundless, and dreams can be helpful in prompting the self-analysis that helps you to see this. It can help if you describe your insecurity dreams to the person with whom you are involved, as friend or partner, as that person may well be prompted, even unconsciously, to give you welcome reassurance. Typical insecurity dreams include losing someone in a crowd, a garment unravelling, or performing poorly at sport or in some other competitive activity.

If it is your partner who is insecure, you may feel burdened by their emotional fragility, which may well have heightened their dependence on you. In such cases your dreams might be claustrophobic – perhaps being buried, wearing overheavy clothing, or being trapped in an elevator (which should be taking you to a higher level but is making you feel panicked or fretful). However, dream claustrophobia can be difficult to interpret because it can relate to any dimension of life, including your career.

Mere acquaintances will sometimes appear in dreams because you are ambivalent about them. You may be unsure of your attitudes and feelings toward them, or of theirs toward you. You may be curious about them, or they may unconsciously remind you of someone from the past who was important to you in positive or negative ways.

Imaginary people raise more complex questions. Freud believed that they sometimes represent unresolved issues with our parents earlier in life. Also, they could represent some of our hopes or fears. Then again, they may personify qualities we admire or dislike, or even different aspects of ourselves.

When interpreting the role of others in your dreams, focus on their appearance and their actions, but give equal weight to how you *feel* about them. If they give you a name, it can be helpful to work on this using free or direct association (see pp.49–50), as it may have symbolic overtones.

Closeness or distance?

Dream Workshop No. 22

The Dreamer

Patricia, 31, has a long-term boyfriend whom she loves, but she isn't sure if she wants to marry him. A lot of her friends are having babies, but she doesn't feel the same urge. She works as an events organizer at a City firm. Her job grants her a glamorous lifestyle — full of new people, travel and parties — but she is starting to feel that this pressured and often superficial life is no longer for her and is thinking about a career change.

THE DREAM

Patricia is on her way to the airport, in a terrible rush as she's late for a flight. It's a Friday night so she knows it's going to be really busy with people going away for the weekend. But when she gets there, it's completely deserted, which makes her panic more. She runs around, trying to find someone to check her in, but there's no one there. Her red leather bag seems a lot bigger than normal and feels really heavy, so she sets it down on an empty chair until she can find someone to help her.

An attractive lady with long dark hair appears out of nowhere and beckons her silently, and in slow motion, toward a door. When Patricia goes through, she starts falling downward. She closes her eyes and suddenly lands with a bump in a luxurious seat, where the same woman hands her a delicious-looking cocktail. She can't stop thinking about her bag, full of so many important work papers, which has been left behind, but she realizes that there's nothing she can do about it as her seat-belt is fastened and the plane is starting to move. Just then the pilot appears and hands her the bag, but it's now only as big as her hand. She opens it, and butterflies fly out.

INTERPRETATION

Travel is a common theme at all three levels of dreaming. Patricia visits the airport regularly. She knows it is a Friday and expects it to be busy, which are Level One thoughts. The fact that the airport is strangely deserted and she responds with panic suggests a switch to Level Two — her fear of isolation may date back to childhood, but her disorientation may relate to her present concerns.

The **Attractive Woman** may have a personal meaning known only to Patricia, but this figure may also be linked to the Level Three archetype who has access to deep inner mysteries — the Anima. She may even represent a wiser part of Patricia. Although the woman has some negative influence (when Patricia goes through the door, she falls), she is a positive symbol overall (she beckons to show the way and serves the **Cocktail**, providing luxury and kindness). Her actions may suggest that Patricia should try to become more familiar with this aspect of her own nature.

The **Overlarge Red Bag** remains central to Patricia's concerns throughout the dream. At first it weighs her down. Once she has lost the bag, she feels that she must retrieve it herself, but the **Pilot** — who may symbolize her boyfriend — finds it for her, indicating that Patricia does not always need to be in control. The **Shrinking of the Bag** may imply that Patricia's work is becoming less important to her, while the **Flying Butterflies**, an ancient symbol of transformation, suggest that she is indeed looking for change and freedom.

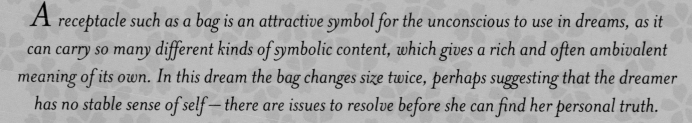

A receptacle such as a bag is an attractive symbol for the unconscious to use in dreams, as it can carry so many different kinds of symbolic content, which gives a rich and often ambivalent meaning of its own. In this dream the bag changes size twice, perhaps suggesting that the dreamer has no stable sense of self—there are issues to resolve before she can find her personal truth.

Morality & Values

Some psychologists claim that we lose our moral codes in dreams. This is debatable. In my own dreams I certainly make moral choices that are entirely consistent with the ones I make in waking life. The idea that we are amoral in the dream world comes largely from Freud's theory that dreams are wish-fulfilments and obey primal instincts rather than learnt social codes. However, morality is far more than a collection of social rules: much of our moral sense appears to be inborn. Our innate decency is apparent, for example, when we feel spontaneous empathy for those in distress. A sense of right and wrong comes naturally to us, and there is no reason why this should not be carried over into dreams.

However, we must be cautious about judging dream actions in the same way that we judge actions in waking life. When a dreamer physically attacks someone, this may be symbolic not of a tendency to violence, but of the wish to be rid of frustrating obstacles. Many kinds of frustration are personified in dreams – even those that do not obviously involve other people. Any authority figure who is attacked in a dream, whether by the dreamer or by someone else, could stand in for a teacher, who might in turn represent new skills that we are struggling painfully to acquire: even if we are trying to learn these skills from a book or by trial and error, our unconscious may well conjure up a teacher figure as the focus for our frustration. Similarly, if the dreamer attacks someone who is elderly, that person is likely to represent a form of wisdom or sound advice that the dreamer has ignored in waking life.

If we find ourselves confronting an enemy in a dream, another possibility is that he or she represents the Shadow side of our own personality that contains the things we most dislike about ourselves, many of which are repressed into the unconscious.

Our values as well as our morals appear to stay with us in our dreams. We may even have the same likes and dislikes as in daily life. But there are occasions when dreamers report remaining indifferent in dreams to the things they usually prize. This has echoes of the indifference that people report during out-of-body experiences (see pp.161-162) toward their own bodies. It is as if the dreamer recognizes the transient, unimportant nature of so much of what passes as important in waking life. At other times an emotionally neutral dream may simply be giving us a rest from the intense feelings of the day. Strong feelings, such as anxiety for those we love, can be exhausting, and our dreams may be suggesting that we should keep more of a sense of proportion. Some dreamers speak of experiencing a form of emotional freedom in their dreams, as if they are setting out alone into an undiscovered and inviting countryside, free of their usual responsibilities.

Guilt is a common emotion in waking life. If we have a moral code and a set of values, we are disappointed when we fall short of our own standards. We may also carry with us some of the guilt we felt as children when the adults in our lives drew attention to our shortcomings. In consequence, we are often said to have, consciously or unconsciously, an imaginary parent or teacher who watches and criticizes our actions. In dreams this tendency toward self-victimization often seems to fade, and as a result we may feel more integrated with ourselves while dreaming. We still have all our strengths and weaknesses, but typically there is a greater sense of self-acceptance.

By contrast, feelings of guilt can be vividly symbolized in dreams. After her complicity in the murder of King Duncan, Lady Macbeth hallucinates that she is unable to wash the blood from her hands, and this is the kind of image that the unconscious might well offer in a dream. Less extreme examples might include failing to wipe mud from our shoes; harming small, innocent creatures; taking more than our share of food; or needlessly destroying someone else's belongings. If you are troubled by such dreams, ask yourself if your guilt is justified for any reason. If so, make matters right as soon as you can; or if this is impossible, learn from the experience and move on. If the guilt is not justified, a degree of self-analysis will probably be needed to exorcise the ghost that is haunting you.

Dream Workshop No. 23

The Dreamer

Robert, 39, works in construction. He has been in several long-term relationships but has always shied away from commitment. He is once again single — much to his disappointment. However, he was recently reunited with an old schoolfriend, and feels more excited about her than he has about any other girl.

THE DREAM

Robert is walking along the street — the one that he walks along every day to go to work — but it looks different because he's walking on his hands, as if this is nothing unusual. Grass is growing up between the grey paving stones, and each pair of shoes that passes makes a random comment, such as, "You'll soon get tired," and "It's all very well, but you don't shine like us." His best friend told him to bring with him the treasure map they found together, but he can't remember if he's brought it and he doesn't have time to stop and check because he must reach his destination by 9 o'clock that morning. He can hear someone whistling in the distance, and is keen to find them, as he knows it's the person expecting the map. But he doesn't rush as he wants to keep a steady rhythm — he's enjoying walking on his hands. It feels healthier than always tiring out his poor feet.

INTERPRETATION

Streets, roads, pathways and the like typically symbolize progress, opportunities, journeys — with some implied goal. This street is familiar, perhaps indicating that the dream reflects Robert's usual way of behaving.

However, this time things are different in that Robert is **Walking On His Hands**, which suggests a desire to change things, but at the same time implying that he may not be going about this in the right way. Robert is also inevitably avoiding looking passers-by in the face, a childish strategy for hiding guilty feelings.

Also, the fact that he is walking upside down may have a hint of immature voyeurism — it allows him to look up women's skirts. **Shoes** are a Freudian symbol for the female genitals, and, as this is all the dreamer can see of other people, perhaps he regards women principally as sexual objects. The remarks made by the shoes intimate that women, naturally, resent this kind of attitude.

Whistling is a symbol of masculinity, but again of a rather immature kind — perhaps hinting that women should be at the beck and call of men, like dogs. The person doing the whistling could therefore be an aspect of Robert himself, while the need to reach his destination by 9 o'clock in the morning perhaps shows the extent to which he puts work and other pressures before love.

The dream reminds Robert that it is not advisable to allow the **Grass** to grow under his feet — he may be missing opportunities for lasting relationships. The **Treasure Map** holds out the promise that a satisfactory relationship is attainable, perhaps with his old friend. But Robert's doubts as to whether he has the map may indicate that he is in danger of "losing his way". He should remember that they are both grown-ups now, and if he offers her the prospect of a relationship, it must be an adult one.

It is not uncommon for a dream to subvert the usual forms of locomotion, in order to question whether or not our journey in life has any elements of absurdity or self-delusion about it. Here the unusual perspective created by walking on one's hands raises issues about the male dreamer's maturity, particularly with regard to women.

Sex & Desire

The appetite for sex is a powerful force in most of us, especially in youth, so its appearance in dreams is hardly surprising – the unconscious becomes preoccupied with wish-fulfilment. But might dreams of desire be more than simply an obvious translation of sexual urges?

To answer this we need to explore some of the most common types of sexual dreams. One kind is that in which the dream either ends just as it reaches a potentially erotic point or is sexually titillating but in a rather tame way. This restraint may be explained by the surfeit of strong sexual images we encounter in the modern world, which leave us little need for them in dreams: *subtle* titillation becomes more appealing to the unconscious mind. Another possibility — especially when we dream of the human body as an ideal of beauty — is that sexual feelings in dreams represent innate **creative urges** that are **being stifled** in everyday life. They might even reflect our spiritual aspirations – a mystic wish to find fusion with the divine. Unresolved sexual dream experiences can remind us of the cycle of expectation and disappointment that can characterize life – reminding us not to build up too many false hopes!

Another type of sexual dream depicts rivalries for a particular person's affections, or conflicts arising from sexual conduct. Dreams of this nature can evoke strong feelings of anxiety, so it is important to consider *why* they occur. These dreams may be an attempt to get you to confront or release "real-life" sexual tensions, or they may highlight the fact that you have to accept the bad times with the good when it comes to relationships.

In spite of the liberal attitudes to sex in the West, the subject is still surrounded by many social taboos, **so it is also common for repressed sexual desires to manifest themselves in dreams,** whether through voyeurism, transvestism, exhibitionism or other similar tendencies. Such occurrences may point to a need to discard unnecessary inhibitions and anxieties. However, they can also be metaphors for problems in other areas of our lives. For example, **dreaming of yourself as a "peeping Tom" could perhaps represent frustration** at being excluded by others in a particular area of your life, while dressing as the opposite sex could attest to a need to develop your masculine side, if you are a woman, or your feminine side, if you are a man.

Red hair

Passion?
Exotic?
Danger?
Temperament?
Special?

Undressing

Forbidden?
Revealing?
Honesty?
Curiosity?
Temptation?

Voyeur

Shame?
Power?
Detachment?
Isolation?
Risk?

Possession?
Secrecy?
Longing?
Envy?
Intimacy?

Mood cues

Discovery & Loss

A recurring theme in myths, legends and fairy stories is discovery. The hero lives in a country ravaged by famine or ruled by a tyrannical king, and sets out on a journey to find a magical object — usually a fabulous treasure or a magic sword — that will restore the land to prosperity and peace. On the way he encounters many archetypal images — for example, a dark forest in which he loses his way, only to be rescued by a beautiful young woman who leads him to the edge of the forest before mysteriously vanishing. Alone again, he travels through a barren countryside to a dark tower or cave, where the magical object is guarded by a dragon. The hero defeats the dragon in combat, finds the precious object and returns to his own land, which he is now able to restore to its former glory.

This theme of a journey that leads to discovery and redemption emerges in dreams — particularly those at Level Three — in various forms. The usual interpretation is that we are born with a

sense of something missing from our lives, something that would bring a rich reward, if only we could rediscover it, even before we know its true nature. In spiritual terms this "something" is usually thought to be our real self, the relationship of our soul to God, our enlightenment, our salvation or whatever term seems appropriate; in psychological theory this goal is thought of as wholeness.

Along with this theme of discovery goes the theme of loss, particularly the loss of innocence we experience as childhood passes. This loss is exemplified in the story of Adam and Eve, banished from Heaven after eating from the Tree of Knowledge — the knowledge that empowers man to seize control of his own destiny. It is also illustrated by Pandora, who opens the forbidden box and thereby lets escape a host of problems that plague the world.

At both Levels Two and Three, dreams of discovery may involve finding a precious object or a secret piece

Mood cues

Reunion?
Surprise?
Relief?
Elation?
Revelation?

Mood cues

Diminution?
Regret?
Ageing?
Longing?
Loneliness?

of knowledge, or meeting a wise person, and consequently experiencing satisfaction or even joy. Such a dream may reflect the discovery of new ideas or opportunities, a new partner in life or sudden good fortune, as well as – in Level Three dreams – some mystical revelation of the spiritual meaning and purpose of our existence.

By contrast, dreams of loss may be about misplacing or dropping something we prize, which perhaps slips through our fingers and falls out of an open window or into a river or between the cracks in the sidewalk. It may be a key, a coin or a piece of jewelry, and the sorrow remains with us on waking. Interpretation may reveal that these events symbolize the loss of youth, or the loss of love when a relationship has come to an end, or the loss of the capacity for joy, which has been crowded out by life's stresses and pressures. At Level Three it may be the loss of ideals or spiritual certainties by which we used to live, the absence of which we now regret.

Loss and discovery are woven into the texture of life. Each moment is lost to us as it passes, but each new moment offers the opportunity for fresh discovery. Dreams can often remind us of this fact, prompting us to search for whatever may be permanent behind this instability, or for something that has the power to transform us for the better.

The experience of discovery or loss, of having or not having, of welcoming or saying farewell, always alters the tempo and tone of our existence – changing it in subtle or blatant ways. If we keep a dream diary, we will see how, over time, our dreams reflect these changes – reminding us that it is no use trying to hang on to things that are lost in the perpetual flux of existence.

Certain forms of loss are permanent – our youth and physical powers as we age, our innocence as we suffer the hard knocks of life, our loved ones when they die. Bereavement can be symbolized in dreams as a physical distance between dreamer and loved one, or even as an image of the deceased in a happy place, reassuring the dreamer that they are now at peace. Other forms of loss are temporary – a loved one travelling, our home when builders are renovating. Dreams will reflect back at you many such times. Your decision whether to accept, to rectify, to adapt or to move on, or any combination of these, is yours alone. But the dream has at least helped you to identify the problem.

Stolen or mislaid?

Dream Workshop No. 24

The Dreamer

Chris, 51, lost his mother two years ago after a long illness. He had lived with her all his life and nursed her in her latter years. Despite his great loss, Chris is enjoying his newfound freedom and even has a girlfriend, but he can't help feeling guilty and thinking that his mother would not approve of his new life.

THE DREAM

It's a bright sunny day and Chris is out walking on the moors when he sees a hole in the ground. Upon investigation he discovers a spiral staircase leading underground, and decides to venture down it. He can hear classical music playing, and it gets louder as he descends. When he gets to the bottom, he finds himself in a magnificent cave full of stalactites and stalagmites. There is a ballerina in a floaty dress, dancing *en pointe* on a large chessboard, which is painted on the cave floor. He watches for a moment and then notices his mother, looking fit and healthy, sitting on a sofa eating chocolates, also watching the dancer. His mother turns, smiles at him and says, "Don't forget the flowers, Anthony." Chris is both puzzled and pleased to see her, but also dismayed that she calls him by the wrong name.

INTERPRETATION

There are some relatively obvious symbols in this dream and others that are more puzzling. The **Sunny Day** probably represents Chris's newfound freedom, and the **Wide Open Spaces** of the moors represent the opportunities he now has to move and breathe freely.

However, a **Hole** in the ground can have many symbolic meanings, some of them conflicting. For example, we can be "in a hole" metaphorically, signifying problems, or we can "hole out" in golf, symbolizing success. A Freudian interpretation might see the hole as a sexual symbol, but there is nothing in Chris's dream that points clearly in that direction. More probably, the hole and the spiral staircase symbolize a descent into deeper realms of the unconscious.

As Chris descends he hears **Classical Music**, and we need to know about the character of this music (is it joyful or melancholy?) and about Chris's attitude toward it before we can suggest what it might symbolize. However, classical music is usually thought to have a beneficial effect on our state of mind, so we can probably at least take it as a positive symbol here.

The fact that Chris's **Deceased Mother** looks fit and well and is eating chocolates suggests contentment, and her smile adds to this impression. It seems quite possible that her mention of flowers and her failure to recognize him are simply a projection of Chris's guilt at enjoying his life. But we can continue to feel the loss of a loved one just as deeply even if we do not put flowers on the grave every week. Clearly, Chris must lead his own life and cannot go on mourning his mother for ever.

Finally, who is the **Dancer**? Perhaps a symbol of his new girlfriend. If so, the chessboard could suggest that he feels that wooing her is an intricate game, like chess. Is he perhaps being too intellectual over this and forgetting the emotional side of any successful relationship?

*B*ereavement gives us some of our most enigmatic yet ultimately most helpful dreams. A dream of a lost loved one can act as an emotional safety valve. The symbolism may be ambivalent and reflect feelings of guilt, but beneath all this is the underlying message that the loved one will always be a part of us — even while we enjoy life's pleasures.

6

Deeper into the Dream World

In more advanced dreaming it is possible to become aware of the moment you pass through the veil that separates waking life from a limitless new dimension. Here almost anything can happen: you may find creative inspiration, share a dream with others or even leave your physical body. Also covered here is lucid dreaming, which is not just a way of having more exciting dreams, but an aspect of inner development that helps us to realize our eternal nature.

Lucid & Psychic Dreaming

When dreaming, most of us are unaware that it is only a dream. No matter how bizarre, we accept it as reality. However, a small percentage of people have the ability, at least occasionally, to realize that they are dreaming and to take some control over the dream. Such instances are known as lucid dreams, and for some people they may be the gateway to more mysterious phenomena, including out-of-body experiences, telepathy and clairvoyance.

Even if lucid dreams happen only once or twice in a lifetime, they leave a lasting impression. When a dream turns lucid, the dreamer typically feels a surge of excitement, and notices colours standing out with new vividness. At this point the dreamer is able to direct the course of the dream, perhaps deciding to visit a distant place, a wise teacher or a temple of learning. Often the dream obliges, and constructs the scene in full. However, the scenery may be different from what we expect, the wise teacher may turn out to be a child, the temple of learning a hut in a forest, and the dreamer usually has the distinct impression that these locations and characters are not produced by his or her own mind, but have an independent existence.

The only problem with such experiences is that, typically, the dream will quite suddenly cease to be lucid: the dreamer loses control and slips back into normal dreaming.

It is possible to develop the ability to lucid-dream by learning to watch dream events more closely. This will enable you to notice the anomalies that indicate that a dream is taking place — cars may be drawn by horses, a row of houses may have no front doors, and animals may use human speech. Progressing your meditation skills will also help you to achieve this. Another method involves telling yourself repeatedly during the day to notice any anomalies that may occur in your dreams that night; also, try to do frequent reality checks when awake, asking yourself how you know that you are not dreaming at a particular moment. Try to be specific in your answers — I know I am not dreaming "because I can read the words in this book", or "because if I look out of the window, then close my eyes and look again, the scenery remains the same". An old shamanic practice is to tell yourself during the day that you will look at your feet or hands in a dream, thus alerting yourself to the fact that a dream is taking place. Once you can perform this action, the dream may

become lucid. Alternatively, you can choose to see a dream object such as your front door or your hall clock. Yet another method is to select a scene or event that occurs frequently (such as being in a car) and to tell yourself that the next time this happens, you will know you are dreaming.

You need to practise these various strategies over many days and months before they produce results; and, as with most dream work, commitment and patience are vital. Once you do begin to have lucid dreams, decide what to do the next time one occurs. Where do you want to go? Do you want to travel forward or back in time? Whom might you want to meet? Lucid dreaming can be an intensely spiritual and revealing experience. Be prepared too for the fact that sometimes the ability comes and goes. We may lucid-dream regularly for a time, but then go through a fallow period — the reasons for this remain unclear, but worry and stress in waking life may inhibit the process.

OUT-OF-BODY EXPERIENCES (OBEs)

Lucid dreams have been known to lead to out-of-body experiences (OBEs), when the consciousness is felt to leave the physical body and exist independently of it. Such experiences tend to happen spontaneously, occasionally in waking life but more frequently during sleep. In a typical example individuals find themselves standing or floating outside the physical body, which they are able to look down on, sometimes dispassionately — as if it belonged to someone else, like discarded clothing. This feeling of detachment is particularly strong in OBEs that result from a near-death experience, when a person is found for a short time to be clinically dead from cardiac failure or another cause. Typically, it is only with great reluctance that the consciousness returns to the physical body on resuscitation.

Reports suggest that once out of the body, the consciousness either remains in the real world, where it may be able to "float" through walls and visit chosen destinations, or travels to what appears to be an inexact copy of reality, the "astral world". Sceptics claim that nothing actually leaves the body: the dreaming mind simply builds an imaginary "model" of the real world. However, several studies have shown how some people are able to interact with the physical environment while out of their bodies. In one study led by Professor Charles Tart in the sleep laboratory of the University of California at Davis, a young woman was able to read a random five-figure number during an OBE and accurately recall it afterwards. A different study, by William Roll and the late Professor Robert Morris, suggested that a young man was able to significantly influence the movements of his pet cat several blocks away while in an OBE. We also have reports from people who claim to have seen the exteriorized consciousness of someone having an OBE – in fact, I myself have witnessed this, and it was one of the strangest experiences of my life. The friend I saw looked so realistic that I was convinced she was physically present. I spoke to her and then saw her gradually become transparent before finally disappearing.

Dreaming seems to be a halfway house to OBEs, and many methods have been suggested for turning the former into the latter. One of the best known is to imagine yourself ascending in an elevator as you fall asleep, with the intention of stepping out when you reach the top floor. Similarly, you can picture a door through which you will pass in your dreams. Another method is simply to instruct yourself to leave your body during dreams, and to reinforce this instruction you can imagine it happening as you fall asleep. Needless to say, none of these should be tried if you are of a nervous or unstable disposition.

DREAM TELEPATHY AND CLAIRVOYANCE

Throughout the centuries, there have been numerous accounts of people receiving news via a dream of the death of a loved one, of seeing an impending disaster that they are then able to avoid, or of gaining information they could not have received by any other means. These experiences all appear to be paranormal, but do they have any basis in fact or are they all illusory in some way?

In sleep the conscious mind becomes quiet, and this allows the unconscious to process impressions that have gone unnoticed during the day, influencing the content of dreams, and research suggests that those that appear to be psychic may indeed be paranormal. Work carried out some years ago at the Dream Laboratory in

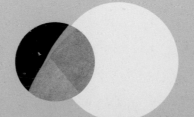

the Maimonides Medical Center in New York involved volunteers sleeping in the laboratory, while experimenters attempted to send them pictures telepathically. When woken to describe their dreams, the sleepers reported things that related clearly, beyond the possibility of chance, to the pictures.

It is possible that we may also receive impressions from the minds of other sleepers (see p.165) or even, perhaps, from those who have experienced the change we call death. This might help to explain instances in which people have dreamed of past lives or apparently accessed such memories during hypnotic regression. Rather than evoking his or her own past life, the dreamer may be picking up the memories of the deceased.

Research suggests that the more we work upon remembering, controlling and interpreting our dreams, the more likely psychic dreaming is to happen, and the more likely we are to be aware of the results. Try looking for correspondences between the events recorded in your dream diary and your experiences in daily life. Do any of the former appear to predict the latter? While it is important not to accept paranormality too readily, it is equally important to be open to the possibility of its existence, since undue scepticism seems to inhibit its operation. If you experience a dream visit from a deceased relative, ask yourself if you had a strong conviction at the time that the person really was there, full of life. Was the dream simply *about* them, or did it convey a sense of their actual presence? This sense of presence is a powerful suggestion of paranormal forces.

Several Eastern traditions, such as Hinduism and Buddhism, insist that meditation can lead to the development of psychic abilities, and there are many additional practices that can help. Start by tackling the anagram problem-solving method explained on p.56, then graduate to sleeping on problems that the mind cannot solve by normal means. For example, you could try to help a friend find a lost object, or try to determine someone's birthday when you have no idea of what it might be.

Psychic abilities may well be an innate part of human nature, requiring only the right conditions, such as dreams, to manifest themselves. People who have these experiences find them convincing and, if they suggest that the dead are enjoying some kind of afterlife, often deeply comforting.

Dream Sharing

The term "dream sharing" has two meanings: the first refers to groups who meet to discuss their dreams; the second refers to occasions when two people seem to have the same dream, sometimes even appearing in each other's dreams.

Talking about dreams within a gathering of interested people can be a valuable exercise, focusing attention on their importance and often resulting in a more enriching dream life for all those involved. Individuals are also able to share information on how best to remember and interpret dreams, and this can prompt the dreamer to think more constructively about both their content and their logic.

Occasions when people share each other's dream are relatively rare and always intriguing. Sometimes they may be pure coincidence – for example, if two people have been involved in the same activities during the day, they may have similar Level One dreams (see pp.28-29). At other times, particularly when two people are close emotionally, something more extraordinary seems to be happening. A woman may dream she is running for a bus, then on waking her partner will ask her if she caught it. Or a husband may dream he is about to dive into a swimming pool and his wife, waking at the same time, may tell him that the water will be much too cold. In such cases there appears to be input from both dreamers, and the dream is an amalgam of two sets of memories, preoccupations, complexes and motives.

Some psychologists have attempted to induce shared dreams. One of the most successful techniques is co-hypnosis, as both hypnosis and dreams allow access to the deep levels of the unconscious. Two people sit facing each other repeating hypnotic instructions. As they sink simultaneously into sleep (or trance), each enters a prearranged dream which then takes over and follows its own course that both participants share. (Work of this kind should be carried out only with someone who is professionally trained and qualified in the techniques concerned.)

Transpersonal psychologists (see p.20) sometimes use a similar method, known as a guided daydream or fantasy. Various psychologists, including Sigmund Freud, have experienced telepathic communications with clients under analysis on occasion, suggesting that in a dreamlike state, minds can draw closer together.

Dream Creativity

Some people think they are not creative or have no powers of visualization. But as our dreams show us every night, we all have creative abilities. Most psychologists believe that creativity originates in the unconscious mind, which continually shuffles through thoughts and experiences until it recognizes something that may be of use. It then offers an idea to the conscious mind, which must edit that idea into acceptable form.

However, many musicians, writers and artists claim that there is more to the process than this, and that ideas may sometimes come from elsewhere. Mozart is said to have "heard" his music as if objectively, and the Italian composer Giuseppe Tartini once dreamed that the devil visited him and played a sonata that "surpassed the wildest flights of my imagination". Although unable to recall it fully on waking, Tartini considered *Il Trillo del Diavolo* (*The Devil's Trill*) the best piece he had ever written. Robert Louis Stevenson found that by telling himself stories as he was going to sleep, his "little people", as he called them, continued the stories in his dreams, creating tale after tale "upon their lighted theatre".

Yet creative inspiration in dreams is not just the monopoly of musicians and writers. Niels Bohr, a key figure in early quantum physics, is said to have dreamed the long-sought model of the atom, and the Russian chemist Dmitri Mendeleev dreamed the Periodic Table of elements – to give only two impressive examples.

In all these instances the writers and scientists were already immersed in their work and were looking for new perspectives – so inspiration may have come from their unconscious, which formed new ideas at night in the process of reviewing recent thoughts. But another theory is that dream inspiration comes from a more spiritual source and works because the dreamer is motivated and receptive. Believing that inspiration can infiltrate your dreams is a good way to encourage it, so try the following:

1. *Identify the specific inspiration you require (for example, the opening theme to a song you are writing).*
2. *Think of the desired goal frequently and tell yourself confidently that it will be given to you in dreams.*
3. *Make no conscious attempt to find inspiration.*
4. *Hold the wish in your mind as you fall asleep.*
5. *Write down your dreams, and work on the possible meaning of any symbols with free or direct association.*
6. *Be patient; if inspiration does not come immediately, tell yourself that it will come another night.*

Dreams & the Spiritual Self

The connection between dreams and the spiritual self is attested by centuries of human experience. From the earliest times, people have reported receiving guidance in dreams from spiritual sources—whether God, saints or guardian angels — often in the form of information they could not have obtained by "normal" means. Such revelations have reinforced our conviction that we are more than our material selves and that physical death is not the end of human consciousness.

Eastern religions, which have explored the nature of mind and spirit far more extensively than Western science, teach that the lower levels of the afterlife are akin to the dream world, in that they are partly created by the expectations, memories and beliefs that we take there with us. These phenomena could be said to form a kind of community — rather like that of the universally-shared collective unconscious in earthly life. Interestingly, these descriptions of the afterlife accord with accounts apparently received through communications from the deceased in the West. All this suggests that the progress of the soul in the afterlife and the dreams we have every night might be intimately connected.

Furthermore, in the East sleep is sometimes described as the "small death", the state in which we leave behind the constraints of the physical body and of earthbound time and space. To progress spiritually, it can help to develop higher levels of dream control, in particular by working on the following three key skills:

1. *The ability to remember dreams and to pay more attention to what happens in the dream world.*
2. *The ability to have lucid dreams, in which we know we are dreaming and can exercise some control over our dream experience.*
3. *The ability to seek the guidance and revelations to be found in Level Three dreams.*

The first two of these skills prepare the way for the third and are covered earlier in this book (see pp.36-37 and 160-163). Other spiritual practices, such as meditation, reading of spiritual texts and attempts to live up to one's ideals of personal conduct, are also closely associated with this third skill.

Level Three dreams and all deeper levels of dreaming can arise spontaneously as dream control develops. As always with lucid dreaming, the dreams will take their own, often unexpected course. For example, if we decide to try to contact a deceased friend, we may see her, but she may remain silent and seem unaware of our presence. Or we may meet people who look at us in curiosity, as though we do not belong to their world. The unexpectedness and strangeness of such encounters will often be enough to convince us that they are more than the product of our imagination, and that if there is another world, we have as much to learn about it as we have about our present reality. The extraordinary experience of dream sharing (where we meet a living person in a dream by prearrangement), combined with these glimpses into the afterlife, may suggest that the boundaries between this world and the other are far more fluid than we suppose.

Tibetan Buddhist traditions insist that to make proper use of such dream experiences, we should train ourselves to recognize, even while they are taking place, that they are still the products of our own minds. Developing this awareness is said to enable us to control our experiences in the immediate afterlife. Rather than being distracted by bizarre happenings, we will be able to keep our minds fully focused upon the "clear light of bliss", which represents ultimate reality and which will take us from the illusory world of form to Nirvana, the ineffable state of pure, unified consciousness. By contrast, Western mystery traditions believe that experiences in the immediate afterlife (the so-called lower astral planes, which can be accessed as we dream) offer learning opportunities that allow progress to the upper astral plane and from there to the realms of pure consciousness.

Level Three dreams, in short, can have something of the character of the afterlife. They can also present us with genuine mystical experience, in which we participate in a vision of the unity and love that underlie all reality. At a more practical level, these dreams may provide specific guidance for our personal spiritual development.

However, even our most profound dreams are not able to show us ultimate reality. Our dreams can take us to the foothills of a far country, but there is always something more, just out of sight. In the distant future more of this land may be revealed to us, but even then we may discover that there will always be further unknown hills beyond, concealed still in a mystery that may be as endless as eternity itself.

Dream Workshop No. 25

The Dreamer

Alice, 67, is a retired librarian who was raised as a devout Christian. Having rejected the Church as a young person, she was surprised when she recently felt an urge to attend a service once again.

THE DREAM

Alice has just offended an ex-colleague by making a remark that she thought was witty but which he found not at all funny. She feels embarrassed but also irritated that he has reacted in this way, as she senses that he has deliberately taken umbrage. She remonstrates with him, but he won't listen and turns his back on her. They are standing near the window in the living room of her childhood home. Suddenly, she is distracted by the white curtains billowing at the window, and she notices a white vase full of white lilacs on the windowsill. She examines the flowers closely, amazed to see so many tiny flowers making up each bloom, and she finds their scent heady. Then a huge eagle glides gracefully down onto the window ledge outside and taps on the glass with its beak.

INTERPRETATION

The dream opens with an example of incompatibility. Alice thinks her remark is witty, but the **Colleague** is offended and rudely turns his back on her. If we guess that in this context the colleague represents an aspect of herself, then this suggests that there is conflict in Alice's personality between a light-hearted, high-spirited side and a serious and disapproving one. Alice is both embarrassed and irritated over this divide, as it makes it unnecessarily difficult for her to establish her own identity. The dream seems to show that this relates to her early experiences, as she finds herself in the house where she grew up.

However, Alice becomes distracted by the billowing white curtain, and is entranced by the white lilacs in the vase. **White** is an ambivalent shade, because in the West it symbolizes virginity and purity but in the East it denotes death and mourning. For Alice, brought up in a Christian tradition, the former symbolism is probably the more relevant. This may suggest that the way to deal with conflict over her identity lies in a rediscovery of her Christian faith.

The **Lilac** is another ambivalent symbol, thought by some to represent spring and rebirth but by others to represent bad luck (some people say that it should never be brought indoors). Perhaps this hints at religion's ability to bring reconciliation — both of the many contradictions within our own nature and of the joyful and the serious aspects of life. Also, each lilac bloom in the dream is made up of many tiny flowers, which could represent the many in the one, a symbol of the ultimate unity of all things.

The arrival of the **Eagle** is a remarkable ending, and there is a strong sense that the dream shifts at this point into Level Three. Alice may well be aware that the eagle is the symbol of Saint John, whose gospel is the most mystical of the four. It is for Alice to decide whether or not to return to the Church, but the dream clearly reflects the strength of her urge to do so.

*T*he prosaic and the profound often meet in a dream. This one starts with an offended work colleague and ends with the arrival of an eagle — a majestic bird with a wealth of traditional symbolism, with strong Christian connotations. When a serious-minded person seeks personal wholeness, spirituality, as signposted in this dream, may be the most appropriate answer.

Bibliography

Ball, P. (2006) *The Power of Creative Dreaming.* London and New York: Quantum/Foulsham.

Boss, M. (1977) *A New Approach to the Revelations of Dreaming and its Uses in Psychotherapy.* New York: Gardener.

Faraday, A. (1972) *Dream Power: The Use of Dreams in Everyday Life.* London: Pan Books.

Fenwick, P., and **Fenwick, E.** (1997) *The Hidden Door: Understanding and Controlling Dreams.* London: Hodder Headline.

Fontana, D. (1994) *The Secret Language of Dreams.* London: Duncan Baird Publishers; and San Francisco: Chronicle.

Fontana, D. (1996) *Learn to Dream.* London: Duncan Baird Publishers; and San Francisco: Chronicle.

Fontana, D. (2007) *Creative Meditation and Visualization.* London: Watkins/Duncan Baird Publishers.

Garfield, P. (1976) *Creative Dreaming.* London: Futura.

Garfield P. (1991) *The Healing Power of Dreams.* New York and London: Simon & Schuster.

Goodwin, R. (2004) *Dreamlife: How Dreams Happen.* Great Barrington MA: Lindisfarne Books.

Halifax, J. (1979) *Shamanic Voices.* New York: E. P. Dutton.

Hall, C. S., and **Nordby, V. J.** (1972) *The Individual and His Dreams.* New York: New American Library.

Hearne, K. (1989) *Visions of the Future.* Wellingborough: Aquarian Press.

Hearne, K. (1990) *The Dream Machine.* Wellingborough: Aquarian Press.

Hillman, J. (1989) *The Essential James Hillman.* London and New York: Routledge.

Holbeche, S. (1991) *The Power of Your Dreams.* London: Piatkus.

Inglis, B. (1988) *The Power of Dreams.* London: Paladin.

Jones, R. M. (1978) *The New Psychology of Dreaming.* Harmondsworth and New York: Penguin.

Jung, C. G. (1963) *Memories, Dreams, Reflections.* London and New York: Routledge.

Jung, C. G. (1968) *Analytical Psychology: Its Theory and Practice.* London and New York: Routledge.

Jung, C. G. (1972) *Four Archetypes.* London and New York: Routledge.

Jung, C. G. (1974) *Dreams.* Princeton, NJ: Princeton University Press.

Jung, C. G. (1983) *Selected Writings.* London: Fontana Books (Harper Collins).

Jung, C. G. (1984) *Dream Analysis.* London and New York: Routledge.

Lenard, L. (2002) *Guide to Dreams.* London and New York: Dorling Kindersley.

Mattoon, M. A. (1978) *Applied Dream Analysis: A Jungian Approach.* New York and London: John Wiley & Sons.

Mavromatis, A. (1987) *Hypnagogia: The Unique State of Consciousness Between Wakefulness and Sleep.* London and New York: Routledge.

Mindell, A. (2000) *Dreaming While Awake: Techniques for 24-Hour Lucid Dreaming.* Charlottesville VA: Hampton Roads.

Ullman, M., and **Limmer, C.** (eds.) (1987) *The Variety of Dream Experience.* New York: Continuum; and London: Crucible.

Ullman, M., and **Zimmerman, N.** (1987) *Working With Dreams.* London: Aquarian Press; and New York: Eleanor Friede Books.

Ullman, M., Krippner, S., and **Vaughan, A.** (1989) *Dream Telepathy: Experiments in Nocturnal ESP.* 2nd edition. Jefferson NC: McFarland.

Ullman, M. (1996) *Appreciating Dreams: A Group Approach.* Thousand Oaks CA and London: Sage.

Van de Castle, R. (1971) *The Psychology of Dreaming.* Morristown, NJ: General Learning Press.

Whitmont, E. C., and **Perera, S. B.** (1989) *Dreams, a Portal to the Source.* London and New York: Routledge.

General Index

Index of Dream Symbols